LETTERS YOU OUGHT TO FINISH READING...

Nipped in the Bud
"This letter concerns a complication of jogging, which is apparently new to physicians but is well known among women who jog: jogger's nipples."

Nipped in the Bud II: Jack Frost Bites the Bullet
"A 53-year-old circumcised physician began a customary 30-minute jog at 7 P.M. Weather report gave the outside air temperature at −8 degrees. At 7:25 the jogger noted an unpleasant painful burning sensation at the penile tip...."

"Big Mac" Attack
"We should like to call attention to a 35-year-old woman who had a life-threatening attack while eating a Big Mac...."

Can the Nobel Prize Be Far Behind?
"How to tell the sex of a chromosome. Just pull down its genes...!"

D0587997

HUNAN HAND AND OTHER AILMENTS

Letters to *The New England Journal of Medicine*

Compiled and edited by
Shirley Blotnick Moskow

Foreword by Arnold S. Relman, M.D.

FAWCETT CREST • NEW YORK

CONTENTS

FOREWORD

by Arnold S. Relman, M.D.
Editor, New England Journal of
Medicine

The practice of medicine is usually a somber business. Physicians must deal with a stream of human ills and anxieties, which need to be sorted out, comforted and, if possible, cured. Tragedy and death are constant companions. Understandably, most physicians take their work seriously.

But the human condition, which the physician often experiences far too intensely for comfort, is not without its lighter side. Patients, their illnesses and their complaints, can sometimes be funny—even absurd. The physician's practice is a mirror of society, reflecting its foibles and fads as well as its pathology.

Physicians find relief from the tension of their professional lives in part through the sharing of their more comical experiences. Without revealing confidences, they tell each other what they have seen. Sometimes they do so simply to share a diverting anecdote, but often there is also a useful clinical lesson to be learned.

For many years, the correspondence section of the *New England Journal of Medicine* has provided a forum for this kind of exchange. We receive nearly four thousand letters a year from correspondents all over the world—most of them physicians. The majority of these communications are serious comments on scientific papers we have recently published or brief reports of new clinical or laboratory observations. We try to publish as many of these as we can because that is one of our prime functions. But much of our mail is made of less weighty stuff: clinical banter, amusing personal observations, doggerel, and general commentary on the passing scene. Since we have the space to publish only some of these letters, we do our best to select the most enjoyable and readable of them. Letters of this kind, when published in the *Journal*, are apt to beget more of the same genre—so we must be careful about our selections. After all, *NEJM* is a venerable medical institution, with a serious purpose. Nevertheless, we cannot entirely resist the badinage of our correspondents, particularly since we know that our physician readers enjoy it as well.

In consequence, the *Journal*'s correspondence section deals with a mishmash of subjects—the serious and the scientific interspersed with the not-so-serious and the playful. New readers who are unaccustomed to our peculiarities are often puzzled by this. They don't always know how to interpret our letters. But our long-time readers do, and so does Shirley Moskow. She has done a masterful job of selecting some of the best samples of the entertaining letters appearing in the *Journal* over the past twenty years. She has arranged them under common themes (thereby achieving a degree of order that has always escaped the editors) and has written engaging brief introductions to each.

The result is a remarkable collection of correspondence on a great variety of subjects, most of them related in some way or other to the human condition as seen through the eyes of physicians. Most should be readily understood by the non-physician, although a few presuppose some acquaintance with the subject or with a previous letter or article. Some of the letters will shock the staid or the tender-minded; many of them will seem irreverent or undignified. But physicians are human like everyone else. They sometimes need to smile at themselves and at the absurdities they see in the world around them.

I think readers of this book will understand, and will smile with them.

SYNDROME-READER'S SCOWL

To the Editor:

Recently, I found a colleague of mine in a dark mood that I mistook for an ordinary depression. Upon consultation with a specialist, I was horrified to learn that he suffered from syndrome-reader's scowl.

"Note the pained curl of the brow, the wandering, fearful eyes, the cowering posture," said the specialist.

"C'mon, Brandon," I said to my friend. "You just need to have a little fun. How about some exercise?"

"Not on your life," shouted Brandon. "I might get tennis elbow, runner's knee, or Frisbee finger."

I had never known Brandon to refuse exercise. "Let's catch a movie, then," I offered.

"No, no, no! Haven't you heard of popcorn-eater's grimace?"

"Intense, repetitive movement of the tongue and facial muscles in response to a morsel of popcorn lodged near the tonsils," explained the specialist. "Some victims have been known to insert a finger into the posterior pharynx and induce a gag reflex."

"Sounds beastly," I said. Brandon was agitated and

weeping. "Forget the movie," I said, trying to calm him. "We'll go to the opera instead."

"Never! If I enjoy it I'll get applauder's palms."

"Painful, erythematous swelling of the hands in response to a bravura performance," said the specialist.

Brandon limped away complaining loudly that his orthotics needed adjustment.

"Your friend is very ill indeed," said the specialist, shaking his head.

"Is there nothing that will help him? What about psychotherapy?"

"He'll never submit to psychotherapy if he's heard about shrinkseer's sputter. It's an uncontrollable compulsion to speak openly about one's feelings."

The specialist was correct. We never heard from Brandon again. There were rumors that he had fled to the Bowery, where he has allowed a bad case of tipper's elbow to progress to doorway-sleeper's hip.

As for me, I sit before a pile of unopened journals on my desk, tapping my fingers, fearful of the next revelation. Finally, I can bear the pain no longer. I return to the specialist. He looks at my hands.

"Procrastinator's fingertips," he says sternly. "Be very careful."

DAVID BATEMAN, M.D.
New York, NY   Harlem Hospital Center

1

MEDISPEAK
Treating Chronic Language Deficiency

Erudite and brilliant though physicians may be, many fail to speak English intelligibly. They are mute-ations, carriers of chronic language deficiency. In their offices, communication suffers; conversation dies. No wonder patients sometimes wish that M.D. stood for more dialogue.

In the classic exchange, a physician responds with a "Hmm" to a patient's "Ah." Yet, any attempt to follow up on such a monosyllabic gambit is likely to be a pain. For example, a patient who questions why he or she bruises easily might hear "thrombocytopenia is not among the reported side effects of cimetidine." That's enough to make anyone sore. As a result, exposure to an acute case of jargon fever may cause even a well person's temperature to rise.

The problem has reached epidemic proportions and no cure is in sight. So what's a patient to do? One patent prescription is to learn the language of the natives. Here, then, is a crash course for anyone who has ever aspired to become fluent in "Medispeak."

MEDISPEAK

To the Editor:

The language of medicine was once Latin. Then, in the interests of clarity it became English. Now, a separate language has appeared: "Medispeak." Medispeak is the language of case descriptions and of medical and scientific lectures. For those who have difficulty understanding it we offer the following observations and instruction.

At this point in time we have learned from sequential interfacing with science-oriented personnel that there is usually a positive feature for using the language of computers. When the potential for integration is inoperative, then the significant parameters of mathematic jargon can be factored into the idea track as an alternative semantic modality.

One should, wherever possible, sanctify the mundane with sociologic suffixes. It is more valuable to have a learning experience than to learn, and a positive interactive ongoing interpersonal relationship is more satisfying than friendship.

We must remember that nouns have weight and that language, like a hamburger, is to be judged by its weight. We should not therefore have patients but "a patient population," not time but "a time course" and not a crisis but "a crisis situation."

We must also remember never to refer to the body simply. Our patients do not breathe—they have a "respiratory status"; they are clothed not in skin but an "integumentary apparatus"; they do not feed but "aliment"; they are not confused but have a "clouded sensorium with decreased mental status"; they do not walk, they "ambulate"; they do not die but merely reach "the terminal event."

In addition to obfuscating experiential realities we can with "Medispeak" enhance the importance of our activities.

Technologists are more clever than technicians. A "critical overview" is so much more "significant" than a mere opinion. "Therapeusis" works better than treatment and a "misadventure" is less reprehensible than a mistake.

The editors of some medical journals have engaged in a steady crusade against the sort of distortions that we identify as "Medispeak." . . . Residents, interns and young researchers are regularly seen to be afflicted by severe "Medispeak" and mistake polysyllables for accuracy. The confusing effect on listeners at these gatherings is heightened by the monotone in which "Medispeak" is invariably delivered.

A virtue of the English language has always been its flexibility. The object of change, however, is surely to make it easier to understand what is said or written and sometimes to add vigor or elegance. The use of words to cloud meaning or to inflate the status of the speaker may have value for bureaucrats and politicians, but similar distortions of language, however ingenuous, have no place in medicine.

ANTHONY E. YOUNG, F.R.C.S.
NICHOLAS L. TILNEY, M.D.
Peter Bent Brigham Hospital
Boston, MA   Harvard Medical School

LEGALINGO

To the Editor:

Have you ever received a letter from your friendly neighborhood tort attorney? No? Should one ever come, be prepared for idioms all their own, which might strike you as quaint, even amusing, were it not that it will hurt when you laugh.

Here are a few excerpts taken from a random sampling of publicly available papers on file in New Haven's Superior Court:

Apparently wanting to make sure that the jury understood what death implies, one attorney wrote, "death is depriving him of years of enjoyment." One attorney, representing a deceased woman, wrote, "Her capacity to earn wages has been permanently destroyed." Reputable, licensed physicians are not referred to as John Smith, M.D., or as Dr. Smith, but as "J. Smith who is holding himself out to the public as one qualified to practice medicine."

In the case of an anesthesia incident, the prosecuting attorney wrote in his brief that the physician defendant "willfully and maliciously assaulted the bronchi of the plaintiff."

Ever been at a loss to make an early diagnosis? Beware. You may some day receive a message like this one: "Dr. B. breached his implied agreement to diagnose the illness properly."

In a suit brought against an orthopedic surgeon who had put a nail into the hip of an 85-year-old woman without achieving perfect results, an attorney's brief explained to the court that, "The defendant is engaged in the business of furnishing such nails for sale and profit to his patients." This disclosure at last sheds some light on how orthopedists earn their living.

HANS H. NEUMANN, M.D.
New Haven, CT   Department of Health

MEDICOLEGALINGO

To the Editor:

Dr. Neumann's quotations from legal papers . . . was entertaining for the attorney as well as for the physician. As one in the medical-legal field, I think it might be worth-while to point out that the lawyer's need to conform to drafting requirements and to provide a written nexus between legal elements can produce amusing results.

No less amusing, however, is some of the prose that has found its way into medical records. For instance, I had some difficulty in explaining to my client, a father, why the record said, "The patient [his son] refused to respond to resuscitation efforts and was pronounced dead." Did the son have a choice?

In the course of a nephrectomy, the surgeon "elected to divide this artery after doubly ligating it." Are such "elections" made only every four years?

. . . I am familiar with medical idioms and nomenclature, but I have had to combine diplomacy and verbal eloquence to tell my clients in plain English exactly what the doctor meant when he (or she) stated that there was a "surgical misadventure" during the operation or an "iatrogenic complication" during the hospital stay.

In attempting to communicate to our professional brethren in our respective languages, we do not always make the message clear to lay people. Perhaps both lawyers and doctors can learn a lesson from an outsider's perspective.

LEONARD A. SIMON

Boston, MA

"DOCKIES"

To the Editor:

From personal observation as well as some negative feedback from referred patients, it is clear that at our local medical-school teaching hospital, and perhaps elsewhere, there is a contingent of hirsute, bearded and occasionally bemedaled and sandaled house staff and medical studentry.

What prompted this letter is the thought that this sub-group has received neither the recognition it warrants nor a proper title. For the latter, I suggest that they be called either "dockies," a derivation from "doctor hippies," or perhaps more pleasing, but derived from an older term, "docknicks."

J. R. DAHL, M.D.

Greenbrae, CA

SPECIALTY SEMANTICS

To the Editor:

What physicians require to promote clarity of communication is greater precision in the classification of the various specialties. Of particular value would be unique pluralizations, unmistakably linking each board-certified specialist to a sort of linguistic totem representing a collection of his or her own colleagues. This system has already been applied to lesser members of the animal kingdom: cows, we all know, congregate in *herds*, and a group of whales is a *pod*. One finds a *sleuth* of bears in the woods. . . . Classification for physicians may be established as follows:

> A *cluster* of pathologists.
> A *blotch* of dermatologists.
> An *apparition* of radiologists.
> A *clot* of hem-onc.
> A *pile* of proctologists.
> A *grope* of gynecologists.
> A *squall* of pediatricians.
> A *gripe* of chiefs.

A *probe* of urologists.
A *mince* of surgeons.
A *craze* of psychiatrists.
A *finesse* of general practitioners.
An *affluence* of anesthesiologists.

And so on. This list is merely a guideline, of course. I only hope it will be of some assistance to those *diatribes* of administrators out there, doomed to roam the land assigning titles and performing other duties similarly onerous and equally indispensable to the workings of modern medicine.

JOSEPH NEAVE

Westport Point, MA

CANTANKEROUS SEMANTICS

To the Editor:
Feeling unusually cantankerous and hateful this morning, I take my pen in hand to protest the manner in which the *Journal* prints obituaries. Almost always it states that, along with assorted relatives, the deceased sawbones is survived by his widow. It is hard for me to figure how a departed man can be survived by a relative who was not in existence during his lifetime. The only theory that offers me any insight is that out in the California hills it is common to eulogize a good doctor by stating that he died before his time. At the final rollcall this provides the only method whereby he could acquire a widow in advance.

Along this line, my frustration is not diminished by the fact that in some sections of this country, for a man to marry his widow's sister is looked upon as unsportsmanlike conduct.

LEMOYNE SNYDER, M.D.

Paradise, CA

O Sudden Death, Where Is Thy Sting?

To the Editor:

The title of the editorial, "Prevention of Recurrent Sudden Death" ... is a bit startling. *Webster's Unabridged Dictionary* (second edition, 1934) defines death as "the cessation of all vital functions without capability of resuscitation," and the *Shorter Oxford English Dictionary* (third edition, 1973) characterizes death as "the final cessation of the vital functions of an animal or plant."

Should the title be "Prevention of Recurrent Cardiac Arrest," or does the *Journal* have its own definition of death?

David D. Rutstein, M.D.

Boston, MA

The above letter, which typifies ten on the same topic, was referred to the author of the editorial, who offers the following reply:

To the Editor:

I am pleased that the title of my editorial startled Dr. Rutstein. A good title should catch the attention of the reader and, one hopes, encourage perusal of the article. I was well aware of the inconsistency inherent in the title, "Prevention of Recurrent Sudden Death." However, I cannot take credit for introducing the term. ... It was used by Schoffer and Cobb in an earlier article. ... Returning to Dr. Rutstein's criticism, he will be interested to know that he was joined by the well-known columnist for the *San Francisco Chronicle*, Herb Caen. ... His comment was, "I am glad they are working on that, once is enough."

Elliot Rapaport, M.D.

San Francisco, CA

RETROSPECTROSCOPY

To the Editor:

"Details of health, with special reference to endocrino-pathy, were acquired from all 134 living and deceased members of 5 generations..." (*New Eng. J. Med.* 277:1385, 1967).

A wonderful advance! This technic offers a great future to internists and diagnosticians. Confidentially, did Dr. Pike help in this study, or does the Mayo Clinic have its own "hot line"?

JAMES M. STRANG, M.D.

Pittsburgh, PA

POSTMORTEM APPETITE

To the Editor:

"Abstract... Autopsied men ate more..."! Southern California does indeed rejuvenate, but now it revitalizes its inhabitants, even after autopsy.

S. M. RABSON, M.D.

Los Angeles, CA

DEVIL'S ILL

To the Editor:

We thought the etiology of the Devil's grippe was fairly well established, but on a recent microbiology test, members of our sophomore class reported two new agents: *Luciferiae claspans* and *Griptococcus haedes*.

We were unaware of either of these and believe this new

information should receive the widest possible dissemination.

W. R. LOCKWOOD, M.D.
Assistant Professor of Medicine
LUCY A. LAWSON, M.S.
Jackson, MS   *Assistant Professor of Microbiology*

NOTE: *When the devil has the grippe, unearthly causes are in order.—Ed.*

GENIAL PSYCHIATRY

To the Editor:

On page 499 of the August 22 issue of the *Journal* I note that a new office is being opened "for the fulltime practice of geneal psychiatry."

If this is a typographic error and the correct spelling should be "genial," I can only say, "Isn't it about time?"

E. Y. DAVIS, M.D.
Lachine Rapids, Canada

NOTE: *Although the* Journal *is disinclined to publish anonymous letters, or those signed by a pseudonym, our photo-offset slips must be publicly acknowledged. Even William Osler would not have approved; he once wrote, "Don't print anything from that man Davis: I know he is not a reputable character."—Ed.*

DOWN WITH ASPs

To the Editor:

I find myself becoming increasingly bew\
the use of acronyms (A) in scientific publica\
suppose the purpose is to save the time (T) o\
writers (SW) and their secretaries (Ss). This is becoming a
silly fad (F). I can say to H with silly Fs and the T of SWs
and their Ss. Down with As. Up with clarity and ease of
comprehension!

BLY yours,

RICHARD DAY, M.D.

New Rochelle, NY

"URETEROSIGMOIDOSCOPY"

To the Editor:

On the cover of the November 17, 1977 issue of the
Journal is an article entitled "Vitamin D Resistance in Os-
teomalacia after Ureterosigmoidoscopy." I hope we can get
more information on this new instrument that allows one to
examine the sigmoid colon through the ureter.

W. GEOFFREY WYSOR, JR., M.D.

Durham, NC

*NOTE: We blush to admit that Dr. Wysor has caught us
advertising a nonexistent 'scope. Fiberoptics being what
they are, we fully expect this device to be invented soon.
However, we accept responsibility only for that one gaffe;
the spelling of "resistence" Dr. Wysor will have to explain.—Ed.*

...ORS, ATTENTION

...o the Editor:

Such might have been the headline if diving had been popular a century ago. Words become popular or unpopular depending upon the fancy, and the word "urinator," meaning diver, is now out of style, but let us look at the books. Here we find:

1. URINATOR—a diver; URINATRIX—a female diver, from Latin, urinor, *to dive*. (This is to be distinguished from urine or urinate; from Latin, urina.)

2. URINATOR (Latin, urinari—to plunge under water) obs.—one who dives under the water for something: Diver.

3. URINA, -ae. F., *urine*.

URINATOR, -oris, m. (urinor), *a diver*

URINO, -are and URINOR, -ari, deponent *to dive*. The Galapagos Island brown pelican has the scientific label *Pelecanus occidentalis urinator*, a label that immediately tells the scientist that this bird is a diving bird.

Because this word is now obsolete in our language, no diving group would now want to be called the URINATORS.

WILLIAM C. VAN ARSDEL, III

Washington, DC

NOTE: Not even pearl urinators?—Ed.

HIPPOCRATIC OAFS

To the Editor:

In the past few years the *Journal* has been the forum for medical wit in the form of sports-medicine case reports, poems, and other medically related frivolity. I would like to present to the readers a word game based on well-known names and recognized specialty fields.

Audrey Heparin	*Coagulation-hematologist*
Sigmoid Freud	*Proctologist*
Barium Manilow	*Radiologist*
Urethra Franklin	*Urologist*
Lues Armstrong	*Syphilologist*
Billy Gram Stain	*Microbiologist*
Psammoma Davis, Jr.	*Pathologist*
Farrah Forceps	*Obstetrician*
Larynx of Arabia	*Otolaryngologist*

JOSEPH SEGEN, M.D.

Bronx, NY   Montefiore Hospital and Medical Center

MORE HIPPOCRATIC OAFS

To the Editor:

Dr. Segen, I have picked up your glove. . . . Not since the days when I played "geography" in the back seat of the family car have I been so inspired to engage in constructive malaprops. Some of my newfound celebrities are listed below. Should the President decide to enter radiology in order to see through the economic haze, would he be known as "Ronald Roentgen"?

Bela Glucosi	*Diabetologist*
Edward R. Marrow	*Hematologist*
Red Skeleton	*Orthopedist*

Golgi Meier	*Pathologist*
Starcho Marx	*Nutritionist*
Nanette Fabricius	*Immunologist*
Babe Tooth	*Oral surgeon*
Gloria Sternum	*Thoracic surgeon*
Edgar Allan Toe	*Podiatrist*
Sir Thymus Moore	*Immunologist*

MICHAEL R. KESSLER, M.D.

Baltimore, MD   University of Maryland Hospital

To the Editor:

Dr. Segen has, of course, thrown down a gauntlet that is too tempting to ignore. I submit the following names to be included in his pantheon of medical (and paramedical) near-greats.

Nikita Cruciate	*Orthopedist*
John Quinsy Adams	*Otolaryngologist*
Maria Callus	*Podiatrist*
Sam 'n 'Ella Fitzgerald	*Microbiologists*
Arthro Toscanini	*Rheumatologist*
Emily Bronchi	*Pulmonologist*
John Jacob Asterixis	*Hepatologist*
Bob Fossa	*Anatomist*
Gingiva Rogers	*Dentist*
Raisputin	*Respiratory therapist*
Zerox Mostel	*Chief resident*

MICHAEL H. SILVERMAN, M.D.

Portland, OR

To the Editor:

We'd like to add the following names to Dr. Segen's specialists. Perhaps they could all work together at Patient Place (in an IV League town).

Biliary Carter	*Hepatologist*
Peter Pancreas	*Diabetologist*
Systole Tyson	*Cardiologist*
Bob Newheart	*Cardiovascular surgeon*
Wyatt Burp	*Gastroenterologist*
Marrow Streep	*Oncologist*
Mariel Hemorrhoids	*Proctologist*
Catheter Hepburn	*Urologist*
Candida Bergen	*Mycologist*
Leukemia Skywalker	*Hematologist*
Stuporman	*Neurologist*
Bratman	*Pediatrician*

JAMES S. PUTERBAUGH, M.D.
CANDY PUTERBAUGH

Portland, OR

AN INFECTED TOE

To the Editor:

A 65-year-old diabetic man had, for about eight months, been seen at our OPD clinics for an infected toe. When I saw him he was obviously depressed although his legs and feet were much improved since his last visit [and we] had little success in trying to understand this man's depression until he said to me, "Doctor, for months it has seemed to me as if every physician in this hospital has covered my whole body with a blanket. They are interested in my toe only. These are some of the things I overheard: 'Dr. would you please see this infected toe in consultation?' 'Well you see, the toe in room 8 seems to be healing well.' 'Orderly, could you take the infected toe in room 8 to the X ray department?' 'Nurse, if the infected toe in room 8 gets worse and has pain, sedate him please.' 'I wish we could get rid of this infected toe because *it* has been here for ages.' 'Maybe a convalescent home will accept *it*.'"

And the patient continued, "For the rest of the world I am a toe, an infected toe. Why can't they look at me as a human being in need for total body care?"

T. SALERNO, M.D.
Montreal, Canada

ON AGGRESSION

To the Editor:

Aggression takes many forms—so many, in fact, that probably the majority pass unnoticed. An important broad class of aggression consists of statements made in conversation that tend to destroy or limit the ethos and creativity of a person, however slowly, or even rapidly, but relentlessly, perhaps the more surely because of the occult nature of the event. Hence, the possible importance of recognition.

Sometime examples:

1. You play so well for a person your age (your color, your size, or your disposition).
2. This is not like you. You usually do so much better than this in that kind of thing.
3. That's very clever. Where did you read that? (Is it possible the man might have thought this out himself?)
4. We oldsters are no match for them, eh, John?
5. I thought your area of interest was physics. How come you are a speaker at this seminar in anthropology?
6. You made that? You are so handy with your hands. We'll have to call you when the sinks get plugged in our building again.
7. We were just going to throw this in the garbage but then thought you would be thrilled to have it.
8. George, you're so happy tonight! You're always

happy. Ever notice how George here is always smiling
and laughing?

9. This is a beautiful picture you've painted. And to
think, you've never had any training; there's no background of art in your family! (I can recognize the thing
that you painted!) (You could almost sell this, you
know!)

10. Yes, this is a Ming vase. Good for you!

11. Janie is quite the young woman now. Aren't you,
dear?

PETER A. McDERMICK, M.D., C.M.
Vancouver, Canada   University of British Columbia

GOING TO FIR

To the Editor:

I always knew the *Journal* was innovative, but the table
of contents of the October 5 Correspondence section, for
page 724, really branched out. First acupuncture, and now
"lumber" puncture! Of course, we've all heard of cast-iron
stomachs—why not lumber spines?

What wood anyone think of next? This is all fine for
sprucing up the Correspondence section, but I hope the
proofreaders didn't go too far out on a limb, or must they
now pine in their ashes? I can imagine the timbre of their
groans. At least the editorial board is on the level, and
won't be distressed.

JERRY L. GREENBURG, M.D.
Los Angeles, CA   UCLA School of Medicine

ON A WEE "WE"

To the Editor:

I believe that in the editorial "The Fraudulent We," the writer overreacted a wee bit. But as far as "urination" vs. "respond to a call of nature," oui, oui!

ELMER N. ZINNER, M.D.

Binghamton, NY

ON NON-A, NON-B HEPATITIS

To the Editor:

Why can't we just call it hepatitis C?

LOUIS KURITZKY, M.D.

Gainesville, FL   Alachua General Hospital

LONGEST WORD: PNEUMONOULTRAMICROSCOPICSILICOVOL- CANOCONIOSIS

To the Editor:

What is the longest word in the English language? Most linguistic scholars would reply with the 28-letter "antidisestablishmentarianism"—a good try, but not the longest word in my dictionary. The distinction belongs to "pneumonoultramicroscopicsilicovolcanoconiosis"—a 45-letter giant, carrying with it all the fury of Mt. St. Helens and its legacy of respiratory disablement.

RONALD H. FISHBEIN, M.D.

Baltimore, MD

2

GOOD SPORTS
Fit Isn't Necessarily Healthy

*Once upon a time, phys ed fizzled out with school gradua-
tion. Adults only exercised options. To jog meant to stir
memory, and rackets were the business of the mob. All that
has changed. The environmental movement is fixated on
waist control. Since the wellness revolution, paunches are
passé; beautiful bodies are now in. Body sculpting is the
latest form of art. To be healthy is no longer enough. One
must be physically fit. Body-building fanatics crazed by the
sports and exercise boom not only endure their self-in-
flicted pain and bruises, they pronounce such a workout
good. Perhaps that's why a chain of exercise salons has
adopted the name Anatomy Asylum.*

*But the best-laid exercise plans sometimes go awry.
Would-be athletes determined to get into condition repeatedly miscalculate what that condition will be. Sports medicine's roster, however, memorializes their mishaps,
including "jogger's nipples," "goggle migraine," and
"scrum strep." "Celtics fever" is evidence that the "passive" spectator also can be at risk. Enthusiastic fans*

cheering a favorite team may find sporting events stressful to their hearts. And, as these letters from the Journal *suggest, when it comes to sports and exercise injuries, the physician's apt motto often is "Doctor, heal thyself."*

TREATMENT OF J-W SYNDROME

To the Editor:

In the snow belt, various theories have been proposed in answer to the frequent question, "What happens to the jogger in the winter time?" Among others there are the hibernation, snow-mobile, Budweiser and T-V theories, all self-explanatory. I personally favor the going-to-pot theory, or, as I have renamed it to conform with current medical fashion, the J-W (jogger's winter) syndrome.

The syndrome is characterized by loss of appetite, concomitant weight gain, irritability, insomnia and constipation. The patient may typically be found staring moodily out the window at the snowy landscape while supposedly watching a football game on television. (Sipping malt beverage may also occur, thus making my theory an actual synthesis of three aforementioned ones.) Naming a syndrome places some onus of responsibility on the namer to find a treatment. This, as will shortly be apparent, I have done.

No, in answer to the reader's obvious suggestion, the cure doesn't consist of running around the local YMCA gymnasium floor, although this may be considered an emergency stopgap remedy. Moreover, this particular treatment may give rise to still another condition, which I have named the flak syndrome and which presumably arises from the frequent need to dodge basketballs, volleyballs, and other assorted flying missiles while running around the outside of the gym floor. The definitive treatment of the

J-W syndrome is far more scientific, based as it is on the fundamental ecologic principle, the "differential adaptive response," or, more popularly, "If you can't lick 'em, join 'em."

Yes, the answer is cross-country skiing or ski touring. Why not? It's really almost like jogging on snow, but easier; the jogger stays outdoors where he belongs, the woods are unbelievably beautiful in the winter, and, as an added bonus, the stares of the curious are reduced to a minimum. One final word of caution to fellow runners and joggers: don't get overenthusiastic about ski touring or you may become a victim of a lesser known but almost equally serious condition, the S.T.S. (ski tourer's summer) syndrome. (I had a *mild* case myself.)

N. A. HARVERY, M.D.

Glens Falls, NY

NOTE: Why not try the snowshoe shuffle?—Ed.

RISKS OF CURBSIDE CONSULTS

To the Editor:

Near dusk on a recent afternoon, I had just returned from a four-mile jog. One of my neighbors, a state trooper, was walking by with his medium-sized poodle on a leash. He beckoned to a small lesion on his nose. I walked over to him and leaned over with my steaming glasses in the fading sun to offer an opinion. I felt a sudden, piercing pain in my medial right thigh. The poodle had bitten through my sweat pants and punctured my leg in five places.

The lesson here is to be wary of giving advice at the curbside. Beside giving the wrong advice, you may get into more trouble than you bargained for, especially at dusk, with a state trooper and his poodle.

WILLIAM W. STOCKER, M.D.
Hyannis, MA

FROM THE HEAVENS, REVENGE ON JOGGERS

To the Editor:

Jogging is popular; it may lead to beneficial metabolic alterations and bring psychological satisfaction. But jogging is also associated with some harmful side effects, such as musculoskeletal injuries, heart attack, asthma, amenorrhea, frostbite, heat stroke, anemia (including that from intestinal blood loss), motor-vehicle accidents, and others. We have observed an additional unexpected danger for joggers: bird attacks.

During the past two years we have cared for 12 joggers, all of whom have been attacked by birds, one even twice. Five of these joggers identified the birds as European buzzards (*Buteo buteo*); the others called them "birds of prey." With one exception, all the attacks occurred during the breeding season for the European buzzard, from April to July. The birds attacked by diving from behind and continuing to dive as long as the joggers were in motion. The victims were all men between 20 and 50 years old. They suffered from scratches or lacerations up to 14 cm long on the scalp. There was always some concern about the risk of rabies.

Attacks by birds of prey, especially *Buteo buteo*, are unusual; to our knowledge, only single cases have been reported so far. We registered in the same period only one other attack (on a bicycle rider) by a buzzard. Therefore, joggers seem to be particularly susceptible. We believe that rabies is not a concern after bird attacks, since rabies virus —at least in our country (Swiss Center for Rabies: personal communication) and in France—has never been demonstrated in birds of prey, and experimental rabies infection of European buzzards has been unsuccessful. Joggers should be aware that nature has its own laws and may not allow intrusion without revenge.

                                          P. ITIN
                                          A. HAENEL
                                          H. STALDER
Liestal, Switzerland   Kantonsspital Liestal

MORE ON BIRD ATTACKS

To the Editor:

. . . Concerning joggers being attacked by birds, my son related similar occurrences while he was cutting the grass. He also mentioned having discussed this problem with other students who had experienced the same situation. They found no mystery to be solved. They had decided that the perspiration on their heads attracted gnats. The birds, rather than attacking them, were only snacking on the bugs.

                          C. JAMES FERRIGNO, JR., M.D.
Berwick, PA

JOGGER'S NIPPLES

To the Editor:

. . . This letter concerns a complication of jogging, jogger's nipples, which is apparently new to physicians but is well known among women who jog.

The condition consists of simple irritation of the nipples caused by friction against a shirt. It occurs in women who do not wear a brassiere while jogging. The patient who brought this condition to my attention stated that she felt more comfortable jogging without a brassiere. She had been advised by friends who jogged that other women also had this problem.

The remedy suggested to her by other joggers was to coat the nipples with petrolatum before jogging. Talcum powder had also been suggested.... The wearing of a blouse with a smooth hard finish (silk, or a synthetic) rather than the usual T-shirt would also be expected to reduce the friction.

Jogger's nipples are, of course, self-healing if further trauma can be avoided.

FRED LEVIT, M.D.

Chicago, IL   Northwestern University Medical School

NOTE: *This problem is also well known among male long-distance runners. They often prevent the pain and bleeding with tape, and . . . they don't think it's a laughing matter.—Ed.*

PENILE FROSTBITE, AN UNFORESEEN HAZARD OF JOGGING

To the Editor:

A 53-year-old circumcised physician, nonsmoker, light drinker (one highball before dinner), 1.78 meters tall, weighing 70 kg, with no illnesses, performing strenuous physical exercise for many years, began a customary 30-minute jog in a local park at 7 P.M. on December 3, 1976. He wore flare-bottom double-knit polyester trousers, Dacron-cotton boxer-style undershorts, a cotton T-shirt and cotton dress shirt, gloves, and low-cut Pro Ked sneakers. The nylon shell jacket extended slightly below the belt line.

Local radio weather reports gave the outside air temperature as $-8°$, with a severe wind-chill factor.

From 7:00 to 7:25 P.M., the jog was routine. At 7:25 P.M. the jogger noted an unpleasant painful burning sensation at the penile tip. From 7:25 to 7:30 P.M. this discomfort became more intense, the pain increasing with each stride as the exercise neared its end. At 7:30 P.M. the jog ended, and the patient returned home.

Physical examination at 7:40 P.M. in his apartment at comfortable room temperature revealed early frostbite of the penis. The glans was frigid, red, tender upon manipulation and anesthetic to light touch. Immediate therapy was begun. The polyester double-knit trousers and the Dacron-cotton undershorts were removed. In a straddled standing position, the patient created a cradle for rapid re-warming by covering the penile tip with one cupped palm. Response was rapid and complete. Symptoms subsided 15 minutes after onset of treatment, and physical findings returned to normal.

Side effects: at 7:50 P.M. the patient's wife returned from a local shopping trip and observed him during the treatment procedure. She saw him standing, legs apart, in the bedroom, nude below the waist, holding the tip of his penis in his right hand, turning the pages of the *New England Journal of Medicine* with his left. Spouse's observation of therapy produced rapid onset of numerous, varied and severe side effects (personal communication). . . .

MELVIN HERSHKOWITZ, M.D.
Medical Center
Jersey City, NJ

LYOPHALLIZATION

To the Editor:

> There exists an MD who jogs
> Wearing his everyday togs;
> Without care or worry,
> 'Round the park does he scurry,
> A full 30 minutes he logs.
>
> All went well 'til December
> (A night I'm sure he'll remember);
> He challenged Jack Frost
> And undoubtedly lost
> As Frostie nipped the doc's member.
>
> Now being a scholarly chap,
> He profited from his mishap.
> He penned a description
> Of this new affliction,
> Which had dropped right into his lap.
>
> This syndrome's not rare, I would guess,
> And more cases will soon come to press;
> I'd say, then, in short,
> That this first report
> Shows the tip of the iceberg, no less.
>
> Now, our jogger's immortalized,
> And always will be recognized
> By the medical clan,
> As the very first man
> Ever to be lyophallized.

MICHAEL SILVERMAN, M.D.
Denver, CO   University of Colorado Medical Center

JUDO-JOGGER'S ITCH

To the Editor:

Perhaps your readers could help me with a perplexing and pruritic problem. I have run or jogged for nearly two decades and have suffered many jogger's ailments, including jogger's nipples, penile frostbite and a near case of penile dog bite. I am also sorely afflicted with, I believe, a previously undescribed jogger's ailment. Twice a week I relieve my frustration and aggression by practicing judo. If the workouts are particularly vigorous, I find that on the next day, as I jog to work and just as the sweat begins to flow, an intense itching develops around my ankles and wrists. This itching then gradually works its way up the extremities to the hips and shoulders. Strangely, the head, torso and genitalia are spared. This itching is very predictable and is related only to the vigor of the judo workout and the presence of sweating the next morning. It is not related to the type of judo mat used, the type of uniform worn or the variety of soap used to wash the uniform. It never occurs after other vigorous exercise. Although intense, the itch itself is bearable. Unfortunately, however, it induces a peculiar one-legged hopping gait that has affected my daily mileage. When the roads are icy, it has brought me precariously close to fracturing my femur.

Perhaps others joggers have experienced this itch and have found a remedy.

STEPHEN N. SULLIVAN, M.D.
Victoria Hospital Corporation

London, Canada

SCRUM STREP

To the Editor:

Skin infections, notably herpes, have been described as endemic in contact sports such as wrestling in this country (*herpes gladiatorum*) and rugby abroad (*herpes rugbeiorum*, scrum pox). Bacterial skin infections in players of contact sports have received less attention. As rugby programs proliferate in this country, particularly on college campuses, *herpes rugbeiorum* and what I call "scrum strep" may be increasingly seen.

At Colwell Student Health Center at Stanford University, a student was recently seen with infected abrasions on his leg; subsequently, Group A streptococci grew on culture. Two days later, he participated in a nearby rugby tournament. Over the next three weeks, three more rugby players appeared with Group A streptococcal skin infections on their legs; two had strep throat as well. Further research revealed that all were in skin contact with each other in the scrum.

Doctors and trainers both here and abroad would do well to recognize the extremely contagious nature of both bacterial and viral skin infections in contact sports.

JOHN M. DORMAN, M.D.
Cowell Student Health Center
Stanford University

Stanford, CA

ARE EXERCISE AILMENTS CYCLICAL?

To the Editor:

Over the past few years, these pages of the *Journal* have informed us of a barrage of new illnesses related to jogging. In this vein, it is interesting to note that when bicy-

cling became the rage in this country in the 1800s a similar
spate of new diseases were described in these very same
pages. Nearly everyone could and did bicycle, and a new
mode of physical conditioning, which has been referred to
as "the hygiene of the wheel," began.

From 1891 to the early 1900s both in Europe and in
America, many medical books and journals explored the
issue of bicycling-related illnesses. A new medical category—diseases of cycling—developed as physicians' interest shifted from acute injuries related to bicycling to
more chronic ailments. "Kyphosis bicyclistarum" was ex-
tensively studied and was more commonly referred to as
"cyclist's figure," "cyclist's spine," "cyclist's stoop." The
possibility of hereditary transmission of this disorder of the
spine worried many. Manufacturers were urged to develop
a "health bicycle" that could only be propelled by a person
sitting erect. Many appendicitis victims were also bicyclists, and it was proposed that strenuous cycling might
twist the appendix over the edge of the contracted psoas
major muscle, contuse it, and lead to appendicitis. In similar fashion, it was feared that inguinal hernia might be produced by strenuous pedaling; others thought that cycling
might cure inguinal hernia.

"Cyclist's sore throat" was said to result from inhalation
of cold air, dust, and bacteria through the mouth, causing
irritation and inflammation of the bronchial passageways.
"Bicycle face" was characterized by a peculiar strained, set
look produced by the excessive tension involved in main-
taining balance on a two-wheeled machine. "Bicycle heart"
was thought to result from the regular tachycardias of 200
to 250 that were said to occur during vigorous cycling over
a period of many years. "Cyclists' neurosis" was thought
by some to result from the incessant pressure of the bicycle
saddle on the nerves of the pelvic floor. As women took to
the wheels, great fear was expressed by society in general

and the medical establishment in particular regarding uterine displacement, distorted pelvic bone, hardened perinea restricting childbirth, and contracted birth canals.

In 1894, the editor of the *Boston Medical and Surgical Journal*, in an article entitled "The Dangers of the Bicycle," said "[I]t is to be doubted whether such a beneficial exercise will perish because a few imprudent persons with cardiac lesions overdo themselves. . . . There have been too many spindly children built up to healthy vigor, and too many chlorotic, languid girls made rosy and buxom by riding, for physicians to be easily alarmed and dissuaded from believing in 'wheeling.'"

Apparently, all health trends elicit disease, which leads ultimately to editorial comment.

MARK M. SHERMAN, M.D.
Springfield, MA

HANDLEBAR PALSY

To the Editor:

. . . Here is a report of a case of handlebar palsy, a syndrome that I believe has not been previously described.

This past autumn I rode my 10-speed bicycle from Seattle to Minneapolis, a distance of 2900 km, spending up to 10 hours a day on the road. The riding position that permits strongest pedaling and mercifully transfers the weight away from the rider's aching ischia requires about one third of the rider's weight to be borne by the palms of the hands. By the end of the first week, I had noticed the onset of continuous numbness and parasthesia of both hands in the ulnar distribution. During the second week I began to experience weakness of lumbricals, interossei, opponens pollicis, and adductor pollicis. Through the third and fourth weeks I suffered progressive weakness of virtually all intrinsic hand muscles. Zipping up my pants became an exceedingly exasperating task, and I had to decide whether to ask salespeople to put coins in my pocket [or] for me to say "Keep the change." Wrapping my handlebars with 4-cm thicknesses of kitchen sponge at the end of the first week may have slowed this progression but certainly did not prevent it. I had no median-nerve parasthesia. Now, after two months of essentially no bicycle riding, I have completely recovered except for parasthesia at the tip of each fifth finger.

Although bicycle literature is replete with warnings about sunburn and sore bottoms, compression neuropathy of median and ulnar nerves at the palms is not mentioned; nor is handlebar palsy to be found in the medical literature. Have I received an injury to which no one else is susceptible? With the current booming interest in long-distance bicycle touring, some readers of the *Journal* may see, or experience, cases similar to mine. And for the sake of my bruised ego, I rather hope so.

DAVID F. SMAIL, M.D.

Waverly, MA

PUDENDAL NEURITIS FROM BIKING

To the Editor:

A 46-year-old man was recently seen because of penile insensitivity. He reported the recent completion of a 180-mile (290-km) bike trip over two days. Previously he had ridden approximately eight miles (13 km) per day. During the entire journey he had used a bike with a standard, narrow, hard-leather seat. Shortly after completion of his trip the patient noticed numbness in the penile shaft. He reported the inability to have and maintain an erection through intercourse. At examination the patient had a loss of response sponse to light touch along the shaft. The patient continued to ride at the lower daily mileage and regained sensation gradually over a four-week period. He has since used a wide, padded seat and has had no recurrence of symptoms.

It seems likely that the patient's symptoms resulted from bilateral compression of the dorsal branches of the pudendal nerves between the bicycle seat and the pubic symphysis. Such compression may represent a hazard of biking and a cause of impaired sexual response in men and possibly women. Added seat padding or perhaps more downward seat slanting is a reasonable therapeutic recommendation.

JOHN D. GOODSON, M.D.
Boston, MA   Massachusetts General Hospital

PREVENTING "TENNIS ELBOW"

To the Editor:

As an occasional partaker of the joys of Longwood's greens in years past, and more southern states recently, I offer a method for the prevention of recurring lateral humerus epicondylitis, or "tennis elbow." This method has "proved" effective in a small, nonrandom and otherwise statistically insignificant sample compiled in Massachusetts, Connecticut and New York.

If one has a "tennis elbow," it can be treated by rest or play (especially with lessons), ice then heat, aspirin or acupuncture, forearm band or cortisone.

After the inflammation has subsided, prevention of recurrence can be accomplished by the isometric backhand. One carries out this maneuver by grasping the throat of the racket with the non-playing hand and then, with gradually increasing strength, isometrically attempting to "swing" the backhand. One can do this preventive exercise between games by simply holding one's hand and isometrically attempting a backhand swing. It seems especially important to do this exercise just before starting to play.

FREDERICK H. SILLMAN, M.D.
Brooklyn, NY   Downstate Medical School

GOGGLE MIGRAINE

To the Editor:

We would like to report another malady associated with the exercise boom. I (A.P.) am a 36-year-old neurologist who began swimming three times per week to combat aging. Two months later I noted the onset of throbbing bitemporal headaches beginning one to two hours after exercise and occurring only on the days when I swam. The headaches became worse over a period of several weeks. I had experienced only two previous migraine headaches, both occurring in my teens. During the third week of symptoms the headaches were preceded by a flickering scotoma in the macular region of my left visual field. I became particularly alarmed when a full homonymous hemianopia with scintillations immediately preceded my penultimate headache. Shortly thereafter, my father (S.P), a retailer of sporting goods, noted anecdotally that his customers frequently complained of headaches associated with the use of ill-fitting swim goggles. I had indeed begun using "Mark Spitz"-type swim goggles at about the time of the onset of headaches. To prevent water leakage the rubber head strap was shortened so that the individual eye pieces fit tightly over each orbit. When I discontinued the use of the goggles the headaches ceased entirely. After several months had passed, I worked up my courage to perform a "scientific" trial. Goggle use again precipitated a headache, which started about one hour after swimming. I now use goggles with a single soft rubber rim that fits around both eyes and doesn't require a very tight head strap to be water tight. There has been no recurrence of my migraine headaches. Consultation with one's parents may provide valuable information.

                                        ALAN PESTRONK, M.D.
Baltimore, MD   Johns Hopkins School of Medicine

                                        SEYMOUR PESTRONK
New York, NY   Richards Sporting Goods

SPORTS, NOISY AND QUIET

To the Editor:

Dr. Nolen's editorial, "Can You Hear Me?" . . . contrasts two athletic endeavors in relation to the distracting effects of noise. One can go farther and classify various sports into two categories on the basis of crowd noise. In the first group are sports in which crowd noise during a performance is tolerated and in fact encouraged: football, basketball, baseball, hockey, soccer, boxing, swimming, volleyball, and track events. In the second group are sports in which the crowd of spectators is quiet during the athlete's performance. Here, we can include golf, tennis, bowling, diving, field events, and even horseshoes. If we now examine these groupings several general characteristics emerge. The first group consists almost entirely of races and contact sports, whereas the second group is exclusively noncontact sports. Furthermore, the first group is primarily team sports, with many participants to a side. Thus, whereas volleyball is a noncontact sport similar to tennis, the team size causes it to be a "noisy" sport. And we are all familiar with the change that occurs in basketball during a free throw. For an instant the game reverts to a single individual in performance, and contact is clearly prevented by lines separating him from the opponents. The result is that silence settles over the crowd (at least when the home team is shooting), and any noise would be considered a disturbance.

These characteristics suggest that noise is more readily tolerated when its effects are experienced by a group of people or when other diversions are present (body contact or time pressures).

RICHARD H. NUENKE, PH.D.
Columbus, OH   Ohio State University

CELTICS FEVER: PLAYOFF-INDUCED VENTRICULAR ARRHYTHMIA

To the Editor:

Exercise commonly provokes ventricular ectopic activity among patients with coronary heart disease. One wonders whether the "passive" spectator in the heat of the competitive hour undergoes psychophysiologic stress that may provoke arrhythmia.

A 54-year-old avid Celtics fan underwent 24-hour electrocardiographic ambulatory records for assessment of ventricular ectopic activity approximately two months after an acute anterior myocardial infarction. This monitoring occurred on the day he watched the seventh playoff basketball game between the Boston Celtics and the Philadelphia Seventy-Sixers on television. Figure 1 shows the grade of ventricular premature beat (VPB) observed as well as the range in hourly heart rate in the hours preceding (11:00 A.M. to 3:00 P.M.), during (3:00 to 6:00 P.M.), and after the one-point Celtics victory. VPB grading was as follows: grade 1, infrequent (<30 VPBs per hour); grade 2, frequent (>30 VPBs per hour); grade 3, multiform; grade 4A, couplets; and grade 4B, salvos of ventricular tachycardia.

Between 11:00 A.M. and 1:00 P.M., only grade 1 VPBs were observed, with a heart rate of 60 to 80 beats per minute. By 2:00 P.M., in anticipation of the opening tip-off, frequent (grade 2) VPBs were noted. At 4:00 P.M. (first half) multiform and couplet activity emerged with a peak heart rate of 120 beats per minute. Thirty-three couplets and five salvos of ventricular tachycardia were documented between 4:00 and 5:00 P.M., with sinus tachycardia to 150 beats per minute. During the final hour (6:00 P.M.), 43 couplets and five salvos occurred. The Celtics' victory

			Grade VPB				
TIME	0	1	2	3	4A	4B	HR
11:00	–	+	–	–	–	–	60–80
12:00	–	+	–	–	–	–	"
1:00	–	+	–	–	–	–	"
2:00	–	–	+	–	–	–	"
3:00	–	–	+	–	–	–	"
4:00	–	–	+	+	+[10]		80–120
5:00	–	–	+	+	+[33]	+[5]	80–150
6:00	–	–	+	+	+[43]	+[5]	80–150
7:00	–	–	+	–	+[5]	–	80–100
8:00	–	+	–	–	–	–	60–80

Figure 1. Emergence of Ventricular Couplets (Grade 4A) and Salvos (Grade 4B) and Sinus Tachycardia during Televised Boston Celtics Basketball Playoff Game.

Superscripts refer to number of events in each hour of monitoring. VPB denotes ventricular premature beats, and HR heart rate.

was followed by a gradual decrease in VPB activity over a two-hour recovery period.

Throughout the monitoring period, the patient was unaware of his ectopic activity; however, there was a direct correlation between his sense of "dread" (expressed in a diary) that the Celtics would lose and the emergence of advanced VPB grades (couplets and salvos).

THOMAS B. GRABOYS, M.D.
Boston, MA   Brigham and Women's Hospital

BOWL-GAME PULMONARY EMBOLISM

To the Editor:

A recent patient of ours had a pulmonary embolus without any initially apparent predisposing conditions. He seems, however, to have had a previously unrecognized thromboembolic risk factor, which may be increasingly prevalent in the American population.

The patient was a 40-year-old bartender who was well until the night of January 2, 1986, when he suddenly experienced sharp, pleuritic, left-sided chest pain without other symptoms, while standing at work. He gave no history of extended travel or recent surgery, and there was no personal or family history of clotting abnormalities. . . .

The patient was questioned further. He awoke at noon on New Year's Day, lay down on his sofa, watched three consecutive football games on television, and then went back to bed. For a period of more than 40 hours, he did not leave his home, and he stirred only occasionally for refreshments. The temporal relation of this extended inactivity to his embolic event strongly suggests that deep venous thrombosis developed while he was watching the "Bowl" games, or soon after. Hence, "Bowl-Game pulmonary embolism" needs to be considered in the differential diagnosis of chest pain during appropriate high-risk seasons.

CHRISTOPHER WALSH, M.D., PH.D.
MICHAEL S. LAUER, M.D.
PAUL L. HUANG, M.D., PH. D.
RICHARD L. PAGE, M.D.
Boston, MA   Massachusetts General Hospital

ABOLISH BOXING

To the Editor:

It is right that Sugar Ray Leonard should be advised against fighting again, but not because of potential blindness if his reattached retina should be detached. Boxing itself should be abolished. In boxing, the prime objective (as opposed to what is merely a risk in other sports) is to damage neurons of vital centers in the other fellow's brain stem by causing edema or frank hemorrhage in the neural tissues, in order to bring about the triumphant knockout. In the process many neurons are damaged, often irreversibly, including those involved in higher intellectual functions. Well documented in medical literature are various kinds of brain hemorrhage, blood clots, and the atrophy of boxers' brains. The punch-drunk ex-fighter is one clinical manifestation. It is past time that the pastime of boxing be outlawed. If the same damage to the brain and retina were being done in industry, boards of occupational health and safety would stop the exposure immediately. We forbid our pitbulls and our cocks to fight; why not out fellow men? In this regard, is not the society for the Prevention of Cruelty to Animals more effectively protecting its constituency than we are?

W. KING ENGEL, M.D.
Los Angeles, CA   Hospital of the Good Samaritan

WATERSKIER'S ENEMA

To the Editor:

. . . Waterskier's enema occurs when the victim, traveling at a high rate of speed, lands on the water in the sitting position with a craniorectal angle of 120° and the legs abducted. In the two patients whom we observed, clinical presentation consisted of sudden onset of diffuse crampy abdominal pain followed by an intense desire to defecate. On physical examination the buttocks were found to be erythematous, and the anal mucosa externally intact. Defecation occurred in the immediate post-traumatic period and consisted of large amounts of blood-tinted fluid. Both victims went on to uneventful recoveries.

Although the clinical importance of this entity is minimal, the intense post-traumatic urge to defecate must be respected, and boat owners should carefully question anyone whom they suspect of having waterskier's enema before allowing them back in the boat.

ROGER E. KAISER, JR., M.D.
DONALD ARMENIA, M.D.
ROBERT BARON, M.D.
DAVID ARMENIA, B.S.
State University of New York
Buffalo, NY   School of Medicine

THE STRESS OF PLAYING GOD

To the Editor:

Recently, my life was saved by a lay person after a mountain-climbing accident. The whole event was over in a matter of just a few hours—about the same time it would take me to resuscitate a patient with anaphylactic shock. The next day, I was back home with my family. If it had not been for that rescuer, I would never have come home again. I saw my rescuer as heroic—and felt toward him the sort of gratitude I have never before felt toward anyone. I was overcome with anxiety about the proper way to thank someone for this God-like gift. I realized that perhaps others may have been in the same position with regard to me.

Being on both sides of this sort of gratitude has given me insight into my behavior as a physician. . . . How does one accept thanks from a patient whose life has been moved? Does the fact that it was a simple procedure or action . . . make it harder to accept these thanks or easier? It is as difficult and stressful a business to be thanked as to thank.

. . . Physicians are frequently criticized for egocentric attitudes, and certainly in many cases this criticism is justified. Yet patients project on us a superhuman power. How can we in our profession avoid absorbing these attitudes, when in fact, we perform some incredibly helpful, dramatic, pain-relieving, and life-saving acts as part of our daily work?

We are certainly fortunate to have the opportunity to be intimately involved in the lives of our fellow human beings. . . . Perhaps the best way to accept thanks from patients whom we have helped is to thank them for giving us the opportunity to help—that may be their greatest gift to us.

BRENT A. BLUE, M.D.

Jackson, WY

3

FOOD
Eat, Drink, and Be Wary

Americans are having a madcap love affair with food. Cooking is a leisure activity, eating a social rite, dieting a national pastime. The result: diet books rival cookbooks on the best-seller list. Gastronomic gurus, convenience foods, and record cookbook sales notwithstanding, take-out is more popular than eat-in. Microwave and radar range, fondue and fry, meals aren't what they used to be either. No less adventurous than explorers of old, intrepid diners tracking palate pleasers sally forth with equal aplomb into haute cuisine, junk food, and exotic ethnic.

And, that's not all. Letters to NEJM document eating forays into improbable inedibles as well as cases in which food, though a necessity and one of life's pleasures, also is a weighty medical matter. Studies suggest, for example, that fat is not frumpy; as they age, fleshy females, in contrast to their svelte sisters, maintain more sex hormones.

FAT AND FANCY

To the Editor:

... Well, then! The fat ladies are right after all. How often have we been thwarted in recommending reduction of obesity by a firmly-held belief among many eastern-European and Mediterranean-littoral ladies? The plump-cheeked, smooth-skinned, full-bosomed, bouncy and sixtyish victims of gallstones, colonic diverticulitis and varicose veins refuse to lose weight lest they lose their femininity. I had thought they feared for the wrinkles and the flab that would follow the loss of the fatty packing beneath the skin. In truth they knew, somehow, that when they lose their fat, they lose their estrogen factories.

LEONARD D. ROSENMAN, M.D.

San Francisco, CA

"BIG MAC" Attack

To the Editor:

We should like to call attention to a 35-year-old woman who had a life-threatening attack of angioedema while eating a "Big Mac." ... She experienced acute symptoms of swelling of the face, trunk and arms, pruritus of the same areas, dyspnea and abdominal pain. Symptoms were relieved by intravenously administered epinephrine. In retrospect, she noted that each time she had had a "Big Mac" in the past swelling of the lower lip had developed.

In cooperation with McDonald's of Montreal, we were able to determine the possible allergens of the "secret formula." ... On intradermal skin testing with extracts of egg, beef, wheat, garlic, mustard, lettuce, tomato, onion and sesame seed (obtained from Hollister-Stier Laboratories, Toronto) no positive reactions were noted. However, testing with gum tragacanth . . . resulted in a strong reaction. . . . Intradermal application of the same material to three normal volunteers produced no reaction.

Gum tragacanth is added to certain brands of food to give bulk, thickness and binding qualities. . . .

In view of the widespread consumption of "Big Macs," we wish to alert other physicians to this hidden allergen.

DR. DEBORAH DANOFF
LAWRENCE LINCOLN
DR. D. M. P. THOMSON
DR. PHIL GOLD
Montreal, Canada   McGill University Teaching Hospital

STATUS STERNUENS (CONTINUAL SNEEZING)

To the Editor:

A 23-year-old woman came to the emergency department reporting a 1½-hour history of continual sneezing (status sternuens). The patient reported that she had been out to dinner with several people and that at dessert time, an intoxicated person had pushed ice cream with chocolate topping into her nose and mouth. The patient stated that she was allergic to chocolate. She had immediately wiped the chocolate from her nose and mouth but had begun to sneeze. She was sneezing approximately every 5 to 10 seconds. The patient washed and irrigated her nasal passages, to no avail; she then came to the emergency department, where it was noted that she had been sneezing approximately 300 times each hour for two hours. . . .

It was reasoned that the sneezing was caused by irritation to the nasal epithelium and the transmission of nervous stimuli to the medulla oblongata by the trigeminal nerve. . . .

The sneezing began to abate three minutes after the nasal epithelium was anesthetized and came to a complete stop five minutes later. . . .

This case illustrates that topical anesthesia may prevent the transmission of the irritating impulse from the nasal epithelium, thereby terminating status sternuens.

JAMES T. STURM, M.D.
St. Paul, MN   St. Paul–Ramsey Medical Center

THOUGHTS WHILE WATCHING A RESIDENT OPERATE

To the Editor:

Just before assisting a resident in an operation, I chanced to read the following excerpt from a book on Chinese cooking (Hsiang Ju Lin, *Tsuiseng Lin: Chinese Gastronomy.* Hastings House, 1959). It was written by Chuang-tse in the fourth century B.C., and emphasizes the use of the cleaver. Much of its wording seems applicable to our everyday problems in surgery, particularly the concept of working "with the mind, not the eye."

Prince Huei's cook was cutting up a bullock. Every blow of his hand, every heave of his shoulders, every tread of his foot, every thrust of his knee, every *whshh* of rent flesh, every *chhk* of the chopper, was in perfect rhythm— like the dance of the Mulberry Grove, like the harmonious chords of Ching Shou.

"Well done!" cried the Prince. "Yours is skill indeed!"

"Sire," replied the cook, laying down his chopper, "I have always devoted myself to Tao, which is higher than mere skill. When I first began to cut up bullocks, I saw before me whole bullocks. After three years' practice, I no longer saw whole animals. And now I work with my mind and not with my eye. My mind works without control of the senses. Falling back on eternal principles, I glide through such great joints or cavities as there may be, according to the natural constitution of the animal. I do not even touch the convolution of muscle and tendon, still less attempt to cut through large bones.

"A good cook changes his chopper once a year—because he cuts. An ordinary cook once a month—because he hacks. But I have had this chopper for nineteen years, and although I have cut up many thousand bullocks, its edge is as if fresh from the whetstone. For at the joints there are always interstices, and the edge of the chopper being without thickness, it remains only to insert that which is without thickness into such an interstice. Indeed there is plenty of room for the blade to move about. It is thus that I have kept my chopper for nineteen years as though fresh from the whetstone.

"Nevertheless, when I come upon a knotty part which is difficult to tackle, I am all caution. Fixing my eye on it, I stay my hand, and gently apply my blade, until with a *hwah* the part yields like earth crumbling to the ground. Then I take out my chopper, stand up, and look around with an air of triumph. Then, wiping my chopper, I put it carefully away."

"Bravo!" cried the Prince. "From the words of this cook I have learnt how to take care of my life. . . ."

GEORGE GRILE, JR., M.D.
Cleveland, OH   Cleveland Clinic

Hunan Hand

To the Editor:

Although recent correspondence in the *Journal* has included many reports of medical dangers lurking in various daily activities, only a few have detailed the perils to be found in the kitchen. Since the popularity of Chinese cooking continues to increase in this country, I feel compelled to report a case of a very painful but entirely preventable disorder: "Hunan hand."

A 32-year-old male graduate student came to the clinic in a state of wild agitation, waving his hands rapidly through the air and moaning with pain; he was barely able to sit still for even a moment. He had spent the morning finishing some furniture with coarse sandpaper, and his fingertips had become slightly abraded. He then went to his kitchen to prepare a Chinese lunch of chicken with peanuts and red pepper (kung pao chi ting). In washing several dried red chili peppers, he noted the sudden onset of severe burning in his fingertips, which appeared to radiate up his arms in throbbing waves and which was associated with a sensation of flushing and dizziness. The patient attempted to obtain relief by immersing his hands in ice water, but this only intensified the pain.

Physical examination revealed that the patient was in acute distress. His pulse was 120. His face was flushed red and perspiring profusely. The mucous membranes were dry. Examination of the extremities was unremarkable except for minor abrasions of the fingertips. The patient was treated successfully with lidocaine gel applied to his fingertips.

Dried red chili peppers (*Capsicum japonicum*) are a frequently used ingredient in Szechuan-style and Hunan-style Chinese cooking. Their skin contains several volatile oils that are water soluble and that can cause severe irritation of

mucous membranes. Because the patient had abrade
skin before handling the peppers, he apparently absor
enough oils transcutaneously to activate dermal pain fibers;
because these fibers are most abundant in the fingertips,
they caused him much agony. Obviously, the use of rubber
gloves in handling peppers would have prevented this or-
deal.

This case clearly illustrates that the need for proper
technique in the handling of potentially toxic substances is
not limited to the laboratory.

RICHARD B. WEINBERG, M.D.
Chicago, IL   University of Chicago

TREATMENT OF HUNAN HAND

To the Editor:

Dr. Weinberg's letter . . . persuaded me to search the
medical literature for a fact, important to the therapeutic
management of Hunan hand, that is well known among
residents along the Texas-Mexico border. A little background is in order. The irritating and flavoring agent in all
hot peppers . . . is essentially insoluble in cold water and
only slightly soluble in hot water. . . .

This brings me to some kitchen lore of border residents
that I have personally confirmed: Bathing or immersing the
irritated area in vinegar (5 per cent acetic acid) is an excellent remedy . . . and usually offers almost total relief even if
initiated 30 minutes or more after exposure. Immersion
should be continued as long as irritation is felt upon drying
the affected area. Several hours of immersion may be required in severe cases. . . . (Cooks know that pickling hot
peppers in vinegar or adding vinegar to hot peppers while
cooking considerably reduces their "bite.")

People handling hot peppers should be warned that even if they do not feel a burning in their fingers, they should exercise care not to let contaminated fingers or gloves touch other parts of the body, particularly the mucous membranes, since the irritant is easily transferred even several hours after the initial exposure. . . .

THOMAS P. VOGL, PH.D.

Bethesda, MD

JALAPROCTITIS

To the Editor:

It has been suggested that the ingestion of highly seasoned foods may have clinical consequencees in certain patients . . . that such foods may be useful as expectorants because of their qualities as vagal stimulants. On the other hand, some have suggested that the ingestion of certain highly acidic foods may cause dysuria. Anecdotal information has also indicated that consumption of spicy peppers may cause burning on defecation.

To investigate these issues, we prospectively studied participants in a jalapeño-pepper eating contest. Subjects included three women and two men ranging in age from 22 to 42. None had a history of lacrimation, rhinorrhea, dysuria or discomfort on defecation before the contest. One was a smoker, and one had cough and scanty sputum production before the contest.

After giving informed consent, subjects consumed as many large jalapeños as could be tolerated in a three-minute period. The number of peppers consumed ranged from three to 13, with a median of five. Three of the participants noted lacrimation and rhinorrhea immediately after the contest. In none did cough or sputum production develop.

One male subject complained of dysuria, and four of five noted a burning discomfort on defecation within 24 hours of the contest.

The limited information obtained from this study does not indicate clinical usefulness of jalapeño as an expectorant. We believe that jalapeños may well be the cause of transient dysuria and, in addition, may result in a syndrome of burning defecation that might appropriately be termed "jalaproctitis."

ANDREW K. DIEHL, M.D.
RICHARD L. BAUER, M.D.
University of Texas
San Antonio, TX   Health Science Center at San Antonio

"HYDROX FECALIS"

To the Editor:

The presence of dark stools can be a cause of consternation to the patient and is made more anxiety-producing when accompanied by abdominal pain or other discomfort. The causes of melena are well outlined in several reviews, along with the usual non-heme causes of black stools, including iron, bismuth, charcoal, licorice, and certain fruits.

To this list should be added the colorings present in chocolate sandwich cookies. In several independent tests (with myself and several volunteers as experimental subjects), the presence of black stools approximately 18 to 24 hours after ingestion of 225 to 450 g of chocolate sandwich cookies has been observed. Variation in brand of cookie did not change the stool character. Testing with other types of cookie (oatmeal, peanut butter, and chocolate chip, among others) has not resulted in the same stool findings, although abdominal pain or nausea or both appear to be equally frequent associations.

This phenomenon may be on the increase because of shifts in U.S. dietary habits, so elicitation of a good dietary history in cases of black stools and abdominal pain should be pursued. Inasmuch as "cookie-induced pseudomelena" is both unprofessional sounding and too appropriately descriptive, a suggested name for this entity is "Hydrox fecalis."

STEPHEN SULKES, M.D.
Monroe Developmental Disabilities
Rochester, NY   Service Office

RED-HOT ADDICTION

To the Editor:

During the past few months we have had the opportunity to observe an unusual set of circumstances in a fellow colleague stationed in South Vietnam. He is a 31-year-old internist with an unusual and seemingly insatiable appetite for small, red candy cinnamon-flavored red-hots. Since such luxuries are seldom available in the war zone he has organized a complex set of supply channels from the continental United States. His desire for red-hots is best demonstrated by his continued need for them after he has eaten enough to turn his stool red. . . . He expressed concern over the stools, but found that by mixing red-hots with roasted peanuts he could increase his intake without having the problem of red stools. This practice of pica has been present for about 20 years, with a gradual increase noted over the past two years. His overall status is best described as hyperkinetic especially during times of plentiful supplies, but he has been observed to be withdrawn, irritable and short tempered when the supply has been exhausted for a few days. Cinnamon red-hots contain sugar, corn syrup, corn starch, imitation flavors and certified food coloring. To the best of our knowledge, none of the ingredients are considered harmful, but we are unaware of a similar pica.

RALPH D. REYNOLDS, LIEUTENANT COLONEL, USAF, MC
JACK L. BRATTON, MAJOR, USAF, MC
DAVID C. LOHR, MAJOR, USAF, MC
Cam Ranh Bay Air Base,   Department of Medicine
South Vietnam   12th USAF Hospital

MALEVOLENT CHOCOLATE FROSTING

To the Editor:

In November 1971, 35 members of the medical house staff at a university medical center experienced an explosive outbreak of acute diarrheal illness lasting for approximately 12 hours. Undaunted epidemiologic investigation has now shown a surprising association between those in whom the malady developed and attendance at a birthday party for the chief medical resident. Further inquiry has implicated a chocolate cake served at this occasion, and it is strongly suspected that the cake in question was frosted with a phenolphthalein compound (chocolate-flavored Ex-Lax, Ex-Lax Corporation, Brooklyn, New York). Medical house officers and physicians in general should be aware of this potential cause of gastrointestinal illness within institutions of higher learning.

CHARLES SCOGGIN, M.D.
University of Colorado
Denver, CO   Medical Center

Cup-a-NaOH

To the Editor:

Previous correspondence in the *Journal* pointed out the hazards of sodium hydroxide in concentrated liquid form to the pediatric population (Liquid-plumr). We have recently had a patient who showed the hazards of the most recent efforts to repackage sodium hydroxide, a risk more likely to affect the other end of the age spectrum. Drano is now packaged in aluminum-foil packages as Drano II (Drackett Products Company, Cincinnati, Ohio). A 51-year-old legally blind woman was admitted to the emergency department with the history that she had mixed up what she thought was Lipton Cup-a-Soup, but to her bitter regret was "Cup-a-Drano II." She stated that she was used to having sodium hydroxide in metal cans only. This wonder of modern packaging seems to make it all too easy for a poison to be placed on the kitchen shelves with foods, and one wonders whether this risk is justified by any potential convenience to the consumer.

DOUGLAS R. COLE, M.D.
Lakewood Hospital
Lakewood, OH   Emergency Department

Please Don't Eat the Daffodils

To the Editor:

In this age of women's liberation, a gentleman graciously assisted his wife by chopping shallots for their coq au vin. He noted that the shallots were "mealy," but he nonetheless ate several small slices. His wife ate slightly less, and their nine-year-old daughter had only the sauce. Midway through the meal, the father began vomiting. A moment's investigation revealed that he had chopped up daffodil bulbs instead of onions.

A call was placed to the National Capital Poison Center for advice. Daffodil bulbs are known to contain the toxic, heat-stable alkaloid lycorine, which is also present in other members of the sub-family *Amaryllidaceae*, such as the narcissus, the jonquil, and the amaryllis. Poisoning occurs rapidly, but is limited in human beings to emesis, abdominal cramps, shivering, and sometimes diarrhea. Cases occurred in livestock during World War II when daffodil and other bulbs were substituted for scarce feed. Poisoning in animals has generally been more severe, sometimes including sedation, seizures, hypotension, and hepatic degeneration, in addition to gastrointestinal manifestations. Human toxicity is probably limited by the early onset of emesis.

The accidental substitution of daffodil bulbs for onions is not a novel error. Two similar reports involving the inadvertent addition of daffodil bulbs to beef stew occurred in 1916 and 1924. The strong physical resemblance can be quite misleading; the daffodil bulb's lack of a typical onion odor or induction of lacrimation was overlooked in all these cases.

In all cases reported in human beings, symptoms resolved spontaneously within three hours. . . .

The toxicity of daffodils is rarely appreciated. The plant and flower, although considerably less toxic on ingestion, may cause dermatitis ("lily rash"), especially in horticulturists. The clear hazard of substituting daffodil bulbs for onions suggests that appropriate bulb storage is not in the kitchen. Please don't eat the daffodils.

TOBY L. LITOVITZ, M.D.
BARBARA A. FAHEY, R.N.
National Capital Poison Center,
Washington, DC   Georgetown University Hospital

Clean Inside and Out

To the Editor:

The following is a true incident-accident report filed in an unidentified hospital. The time and patient's name are fictitious. (This did not occur at the University of Washington or in Seattle).

"To: Chief, Nursing Service

"Name of Individual Involved: Smith, John

"Mr. Smith on 14 April 66 was given some liq pHiso-Hex soap so he could take a shower before going *(sic)* to surgery. Instead of taking a shower c pHisoHex he drank it. Because he didn't go to surgery on 14 April Mr. Smith was given some more liq pHisoHex so he could take a shower before going to surgery, but instead he drank it again. There was another person with Mr. Smith this AM when the aide gave him the pHisoHex and heard me tell him to take a shower c pHisoHex soap. This AM the patient complained that the medicine made him vomit to the doctor."

NORMAN R. ZINNER, M.D.
Assistant Professor
Department of Urology
University of Washington
School of Medicine

Seattle, WA

Gastronomically Speaking: Kiszka is not Kish-ke

To the Editor:

Bakshi et al., in their report on sausage cyanosis due to eating kiszka . . . implied that kiszka and kish-ke were the same food product. They should have been more discerning. Although the Polish word kiszka and the Yiddish word kish-ke both literally mean gut, the similarity in the foods bearing these names ends there. Whereas the Polish kiszka is made with the use of hog intestines as a casing stuffed with pork, coarse cereal and sodium-nitrite and nitrate, the Yiddish kish-ke, also known as stuffed derma, obviously does not contain pork but is made with beef intestine prepared only with seasoning, shortening and cereal or grain stuffing. Nitrites and nitrates are not added. Therefore the kish-ke eating public and the physicians who treat this ethnic group need not fear the development of methemoglobin and cyanosis. However, the consumption of kish-ke is not without danger: heartburn is a frequent complication.

MARVIN E. LEVIN, M.D.
Assistant Professor of Clinical Medicine
Washington University
St. Louis, MO   School of Medicine

AROMA OF CHICKEN SOUP

To the Editor:

I am afraid that Dr. Schatz's plea to keep chicken noodle soup out of the laboratory comes too late (December 19, 1968). At the risk of upsetting his mother, I must report that chicken soup has been investigated. It appears that hydrogen sulfide is a major contributor to the unique flavor of chicken soup. Perhaps in a pinch, Mrs. Schatz could substitute rotten eggs in her cold regimen.

JOHN R. SELLMAN, M.D.
University of California
San Francisco, CA   Medical Center

RED NO. "INSECT ESSENCE"

To the Editor:

. . . As a pharmacist, my knowledge extends not only to just synthetic pharmacologic agents but also to natural substances relevant to the ancient discipline of pharmacognosy.

As my spoon scraped out the last traces of a delicious "All Natural Black Cherry Flavored Yogurt," I happened to glance at the list imprinted on the container of what I thought were wholesome, nutritious ingredients. The word cochineal caught my eye, and simultaneously a wave of nausea hit my stomach. Cochineal, I remembered, was an insect. I looked further, and my fears were substantiated.

. . . The whole dead, bloated female insects, some of which contain hatched larvae, some eggs, are used as a red dye. . . . In the use of the cochineal insect as a food dye modern man is no more distinguished than the ancient Egyptians, who fed skinned mice to their desperately ill children in the hope their lives would be saved, and who prepared dyes from tapeworms.

Indeed, the FDA permits an extract of cochineal to be used as a food color but, in recognition of its inherently filthy nature, specifies treatment to destroy contaminating salmonella micro-organisms although the FDA standard fails to mention other bacteria that may not be sensitive to and are not killed by pasteurization. The severe gastrointestinal disturbances induced by the salmonella bacillus and its endotoxin are well known, and what better substrate can there be than yogurt?

The so-called "dangers" in the use of synthetic, highly purified chemicals may be only in that we know them too well. Alas! We do not know the dangers of material of natural origin.

                                     H. I. SILVERMAN, D.SC.
Boston, MA   Massachusetts College of Pharmacy

Martini Toothpick Warning

To the Editor:

We are writing to call attention to a new and potentially serious hazard associated with the hasty ingestion of martinis (or indeed Gibsons, as in the present case). One of us was partaking of a Gibson (gin, ice, essence of vermouth, and several cocktail onions speared on a flat wooden toothpick). As the beverage and onions were quickly consumed, the toothpick floated from the glass into the oral cavity and lodged, uncomfortably, in the posterior pharynx. An attempt to dislodge it by regurgitation resulted in transferring it up into the posterior nares, pointed end first. A trip to the emergency room brought the first author of this letter into contact with the second. Actually, this meeting occurred one hour later, after several encounters with other hospital personnel, who took the history by asking such questions as: "You have a toothpick caught where?" "Are you the man with a toothpick up his nose?" "This couldn't happen —why didn't the olive stop it?" Fortunately, the adroit second author was able to extract the offending obstruction deftly with an alligator forceps. The first author was sent home with the suggestion that he have a drink, sans toothpick. We caution imbibers to consider this potential danger at the end of a difficult day.

Daniel Malamud, Ph.D.
University of Pennsylvania
Mary Harlan Murphy, M.D.
Philadelphia, PA   Lankenau Hospital

Club Med Dermatitis

To the Editor:

The romantic lure of singles' travel clubs includes ensured social interaction through group activities. A drinking game on a Carribean Club Med vacation led to a distinctive presentation of a well-defined phototoxic dermatitis.

A tan 18-year-old Hispanic woman reported a tender rash on both thighs, which began one day after her return home from such a vacation. . . . Her trip had included a drinking game during which participants would balance and roll limes up and down their laps and closed thighs.

Phytophototoxic reactions from high concentrations of natural furocoumarin in many fruits, vegetables, and plants (celery, parsley, limes, and other citrus fruits) peak about 48 hours after exposure to light . . . and resolve over 7 to 14 days. . . .

Phytophototoxic dermatitis is a well-established hazard among citrus and produce workers, but more obscure outbreaks have recently been reported, such as one that occurred among children making pomanders from limes into which cloves had been inserted. . . .

Because melanin serves as a filter, and possibly as a trap for free radicals, phototoxic reactions, unlike photoallergic reactions, rarely occur in dark-skinned persons, except in the case of a mild reaction to furocoumarins, which was demonstrated in this Hispanic vacationer.

WAIN WHITE, M.D.
New York, NY   New York University Medical Center

NATIONAL PREJUDICE

To the Editor:

During the past months, the *Journal* has carried many letters about alcohol and nicotine, as well as editorials on the touchy subjects. In spite of the good intentions of our medical fraternity to stop these two killers, the general attitude is very well summed up by a conversation I heard recently at the famous Munich Oktober Fest. A somewhat oversaturated German-speaking Fester sat down and asked for a Schnapps. The waitress indignantly spouted, "Don't you know that alcohol kills 100,000 Germans a year?"

The Tipsy Tippler replied with perfect indifference, "I don't give a d—n! I'm an *Austrian!*"

KENNETH LANE, M.D.
Spiegelberg/Wuerttemberg, Germany

FESTSPIEL

To the Editor:

Last November the *Journal* published my short contribution to the problem of alcoholism based on an observation made at Munich's famous Oktober Fest. This year I wish to report my observation on the same subject made at the nearly as famous Volksfest in Stuttgart, a huge wine and beer fest held in huge tents. Owing to lack of room, I was obliged to sit at a table obviously composed of full-time drinkers, all red nosed and bleary eyed. An elderly lady, apparently of the Salvation Army, came to our table and held a harangue on the evils of drink, ending with: "I warn you before it is too late! Alcohol kills, slowly but surely!" The apparent spokesman of the group, heavy-tongued, drawled, "So what? We're in no hurry!"

KENNETH LANE, M.D.
Spiegelberg, Germany

4

CHILDREN
Frailties of Youth

The frailties of youth have an advantage over the infirmities of old age: they're almost always outgrown. Childhood is the time when starry-eyed innocents adapt to the world and master a complicated survival course. Control of bodily functions, how to communicate, mobility—all have to be learned. Often, lessons are confusing, so attempts to cope may be funny, frustrating, sometimes injurious. Eating hot foods without getting scalded, enjoying frozen foods and not suffering frostbite, moving about easily in too tight jeans and unlaced shoes are acquired skills. They require practice. Mishaps are inevitable. In many respects, launching a baby into the contemporary world is a lot like preparing an astronaut to land on the moon.

MALE CHAUVINISTS PLOT MATERNAL BONDS

To the Editor:

The study by Klaus et al. . . . is particularly pertinent in view of the movement for Women's Liberation. Is it possible that a part of the impetus for this movement stemmed from the increased number of infants delivered in hospitals rather than at home? In the latter circumstance mothers might become more attached to their offspring and have less time for, and interest in, the "outside world." In any case the way seems to be clearly indicated to male chauvinists who would maintain their "superiority," to wit:

The ultimate weapon is now brought to light
By Klaus and his group in the *Journal*.
The blow that will help every male win the fight
To keep his wench tame and maternal.

The plan, well laid out while the wife's lying in,
Needs only the help of the nurses
To put Mom with baby in nothing but skin
While putting some bribes in their purses.

In a very short time we can modify Ma
With an increased attachment to baby.
She'll ne'er leave her offspring, much less burn her bra.
We'll be male pigs on top again. Maybe.

RICHARD A. ROSEN, M.D.
Mt. Vernon, NY

THE SUCCUSSION SPLASH
AS AN INFANT "BURP" SIGN

To the Editor:

Modern medicine is truly amazing, with the new noninvasive technology of CAT scans, ultrasound, radionuclide imaging, and nuclear magnetic resonance. With these devices we can often find disease in the deepest recesses of our bodies. Despite these wonderful advances there are some physicians who remain disciples of the art of physical diagnosis. It is to such colleagues that we nostalgically wish to relate this anecdote.

While aggressively but unsuccesssfully trying to rock our first child to sleep after a 2:00 A.M. feeding, we felt a gurgling splash in her abdomen. Worriedly, we checked Hamilton Bailey's book on physical diagnosis and found that this was a succussion splash indicative of bowel obstruction. Before we could arouse a pediatrician, our daughter burped, the sign disappeared, and she soon fell fast asleep. Intrigued by these events, we refined our technique at a subsequent feeding. Placing one hand on the stomach and one on the back, we gently jiggled her and felt the same gurgling splash. This splash, which is similar to the splashing in a half-empty jug of milk that is shaken, completely disappeared after the baby burped. With a little practice we could easily determine whether she had burped. From that time on, night feedings were a very efficient process, limiting the post-feeding burping to a minimum from the usual empiric time of 20 to 30 minutes. We were so delighted with this sign that we had three more children to document its value adequately in a prospective nonrandomized fashion.

Since it is unlikely that ultrasound will ever be a household item, we recommend this physical sign to all those who burp babies, expecially at night. In fact, a good night's sleep may save your residency, as well as your patience and your patients.

WALLEY J. TEMPLE, M.D.
DOREEN H. FARLEY (TEMPLE), B.SC., B.ED.
University of Miami
Miami, FL   School of Medicine

Tympany in Traube's Space As an Infant "Burp" Sign

To the Editor:

Dr. and Mrs. Temple deserve congratulations on their use of the succussion splash as [an] infant "burp" sign. . . . This sign may save harried parents countless hours of trying to "burp" their crying child when in fact no burp could possibly be forthcoming. It could also redirect their efforts to more appropriate therapy.

. . . We also discovered a useful sign that served us well with each of our three children. We found that tympany of Traube's space would disappear in the child after we successfully induced a burp. Like the succussion splash, this suggested that the air in the stomach had disappeared. Traube's space is bound medially by the left edge of the liver, laterally by the medial edge of the spleen, and superiorly by the lower border of the heart. The advantage of this sign over the succussion splash is that it does not require the vigorous shaking of a crying infant. A negative succussion-splash sign leaves one in doubt about whether the infant has indeed been jiggled sufficiently. It is relatively easy, however, for a trained person to determine whether Traube's space is tympanitic or dull.

JOAN ZIDULKA, M.D.
ARNOLD ZIDULKA, M.D.
Montreal, Canada   McGill University

Listen!

To Editor:

A complaint of temporary deafness by a young mother (C.S.B.) after an outburst of screaming by an 11-month-old infant (J.A.B.) prompted one of us (L.E.S.) to measure sound intensity during episodes of spontaneous screaming by the infant.

Measurements were made approximately 15 cm from the infant (the distance from an infant's mouth to a parent's ear when the infant is held) during episodes of spontaneous screaming, using a Decibels Sound Level Meter. . . . The As scale, which approximates the intensity appreciated by the human ear, was used for readings.

Much to our amazement, peak readings ranged from 100 to 117 dB(A), with a geometric mean of 108 (n = 6). For comparison, a pneumatic hammer at 1 m produces 120 dB(A); a car horn at 5 m, 100 dB(A); and normal conversation at 1 m, 70 dB(A). Since the scale is logarithmic, 117 dB(A) represents a sound level approximately 30 times louder than normal conversation. . . .

BRUCE BOSTROM, M.D.
CHARLENE SWANSON BOSTROM, B.A.
J. ANDERS BOSTROM
Minneapolis, MN   University of Minnesota

LOREN E. SWANSON, B.E.E.
Minneapolis, MN   Central Engineering Company

AUTOSOMAL DOMINANT TRANSMISSION OF THE "PHOTIC SNEEZE REFLEX"

To the Editor:

Sneezing in response to bright light is a common yet poorly documented phenomenon. In the only major epidemiologic study ever performed, Everett called this entity the "photic sneeze reflex" and found it to be present in 23 per cent of the medical students at Johns Hopkins. Despite its ubiquity, no mention of this reflex can be found in any current medical or neurologic textbook. In a poll of 25 neurologists at the Johns Hopkins Hospital, we found the photic sneeze reflex to be present in 36 per cent. However, only 8 per cent of the respondents knew that such a specific reflex existed. The lack of knowledge by neurologists was surprising considering that the reflex is presumably mediated by the central nervous system.

We now report a documented family history of the photic sneeze reflex. In the index patient (S.J.P.) movement from an indoor location to bright sunlight invariably results in two sneezes. This phenomenon is also present in the father and brother of the index patient but is absent in his mother and wife. The current interest in the reflex developed after the birth of the index patient's daughter (L.A.P.). It was first noticed when the child was approximately four weeks of age that she would sneeze (twice) when moved into bright sunlight. This response has persisted over the past six months. This father-to-daughter inheritance of the photic sneeze reflex strongly suggests an autosomal dominant pattern of genetic transmission. We hope that additional studies will further clarify why many of us sneeze uncontrollably when we enter the great outdoors.

STEPHEN J. PEROUTKA, M.D., PH.D.
Baltimore, MD   The Johns Hopkins Hospital

Towson, MD   LAURA A. PEROUTKA

PRACTICAL POINT ON POPSICLES

To the Editor:

. . . I was perplexed by a peculiar, papular, well circumscribed hyperpigmented area that was present just lateral to the corner of my daughter's mouth on the right side. The dermatitis responded poorly to the copious soap and water therapy, as well as topical alcohol.

While thumbing through the *Journal*, I was startled by a photograph, which strikingly resembled the previously described lesion. In retrospect I remembered my daughters having been on a recent popsicle "kick." When confronted by the question of how do you eat a popsicle, Mary graphically demonstrated by holding a pencil directly over the involved area. When questioned why she didn't eat the popsicle in a more conventional fashion, she replied that it tickled her teeth. Obviously, the coldness produced an unpleasant sensation in her newly forming central incisors.

The appropriateness of this article obviated a trip to the neighborhood dermatologist, and also demonstrated vividly that medical literature can be applied in a very personal fashion.

JOSEPH T. SEMBROT, M.D.

Allentown, PA

FRENCH VANILLA FROSTBITE

To the Editor:

An 18-month-old girl was noted by her babysitter to have extensive "cold sores" on her lips. Two days earlier the child had been shopping with her father, who purchased her first French vanilla ice-cream cone. She ate the ice cream enthusiastically for 30 minutes, never removing her mouth from the delightful treat. When the child returned home, her mother noted swollen, dusky, and warm upper and lower lips. Over the next 24 to 48 hours the affected areas progressed in a manner typical of a local frostbite, with blistering occurring on both the upper and lower lips. The lesions crusted and healed without incident or notice able discomfort over the ensuing seven days.

We are aware of the local cold injury known as popsicle panniculitis, which is characterized by a subcutaneous nodule occurring in young children several days after they come in contact with cold objects. The phenomenon described in our child may have been an extension of this type of lesion, with the initial event being cold-induced anesthesia of the lips, followed by freezing of the tissue in prolonged contact with the cold object. These cold sores were truly sores from the cold.

LANCE R. PETERSON, M.D.
Minneapolis, MN Veterans Administration Medical Center

LOANN C. PETERSON, M.D.
Minneapolis, MN   Hennepin County Medical Center

ANJA K. PETERSON

ABORTION AND TONSILLECTOMY

To the Editor:

Let us persuade our legislators to repeal laws restricting abortion and replace them with laws restricting tonsillectomy.

For an opener, may I submit: no child shall be subjected to a tonsillectomy unless the procedure is necessary to preserve the life of the mother.

HAROLD J. JONES, M.D.
Ponca City, OK

NONSEXUAL TRANSMISSION OF GONORRHEA TO A CHILD

To the Editor:

Gonorrhea in children has heretofore been considered prima facic evidence of sexual abuse. We report a case of accidental, nonsexual transmission to a child.

The mother of a three-year-old boy worked as a microbiology laboratory technician. Each day, she visited physicians' offices within our county to collect cultures. One day she was making her rounds, with her son also riding in the car. After making a number of pickups, she stopped at a store and purchased some groceries. She then drove home, parked, and went inside to drop off the groceries, leaving her son in the car. The child promptly got out of his seat and crawled into the back seat, where the culture plates were being carried. The mother returned to find that her son had eaten most of an appetizing culture dish containing chocolate agar. . . .

The mother promptly took her child to the family pediatrician. Since the remnants of the half-eaten agar grew *Neisseria gonorrhoeae*, we elected to observe the child and obtain specimens for culture. Throat specimens obtained at one, two, four, and six days after ingestion were negative, but a sample obtained at eight days was positive. . . . The boy was treated, according to a Centers for Disease Control schedule. . . . Therapy produced a prompt cure. . . .

. . . San Antonio has since enacted a law prohibiting parents from leaving children unattended in parked cars. The law was designed to prevent heat stress during Texas summers, but this case illustrates that there are other hazards as well.

HENRY J. LIPSITT, M.D.
A.J. PARMET, M.D., M.P.H.

San Antonio, TX

ASSAULT WITH BATTERY

To the Editor:

A child with ear pain of acute onset is a daily occurrence in a family physician's or pediatrician's office. Occasionally, these cases turn out to have unusual and potentially dangerous causes.

On February 3 a six-year-old boy presented with pain in the right ear of eight hours' duration. He had had mild coryza the week before. His right tympanic membrane was injected and retracted. Amoxicillin was prescribed. Six days later the child's mother reported that there had been several days of pain relief but then a severe recurrence. Examination revealed a markedly swollen canal filled with pus. The swelling blocked visualization of the tympanic membrane. Antibacterial drops containing hydrocortisone were prescribed. After a day the child had almost complete relief from the pain. On February 16 the mother found a button battery (from a watch) coming from the child's ear. The child reported that he had placed it in the canal (on February 4) to have a "bionic ear." . . .

Multiple cases of button-battery ingestion causing esophageal erosion have been reported. In the case described above, severe sequelae resulted from placement of a miniature battery in the external auditory canal. A small, smooth object placed in the external auditory canal without undue mechanical trauma would generally go relatively unnoticed. However, the severe erosive nature of the alkaline contents of these batteries (silver oxide, mercuric oxide, or manganese dioxide) makes them surprisingly pathogenic in certain circumstances. Considering the rapid growth of the microcalculator and electronics industry, this diagnosis may need to be considered more often in the future.

LESLIE S. RACHLIN, M.D

Pine City, NY

MORE NOISE IN THE EAR CANAL

To the Editor:

I was ten years old, living in Guyana, and I had had no previous ear problem. I was awakened one night in bed by a thundering noise and severe pain in the left ear. The noise came in waves and was accompanied by nausea. When repeated tugging and slapping of the pinna failed to relieve the noise, I had the idea of "drowning out" the noise. I filled the ear canal with tap water. The noise immediately became distant, then over a period that seemed like ages, but was probably 10 minutes, it became less frequent and stopped. I mopped the ear canal with the corner of a Kleenex and was surprised to extract a dead ant. . . .

KEN YONG-HING, M.D.
Saskatoon, Canada   University Hospital

CHASING THE DOLLAR—A CASE REPORT

To the Editor:

Ingested foreign bodies are commonly seen in emergency-room practice and usually pass harmlessly along the gastrointestinal tract. Occasionally, however, the physician must act to remove them because obstruction, perforation or bleeding is threatened. . . .

A 16-year-old boy complained that he had accidentally swallowed a half dollar, five days before. He was concerned because it had not passed in his stools. He was asymptomatic, and physical examination was unremarkable. Abdominal radiographs showed a round, metallic, foreign body in the stomach. An attempt at endoscopic removal was agreed upon. . . .

The Olympus GIF fiberoptic esophagogastroduodenoscope was passed with ease, and when the stomach was entered, it became obvious that there were two half dollars lying back to back. The Cameron-Miller polypectomy snare was used to hook the coins, and they were brought easily and atraumatically out of the stomach. The procedure took 10 minutes, and the patient tolerated it well. He went home after an hour.

JEFFREY L. PONSKEY, M.D.
Cleveland, OH   University Hospitals of Cleveland

JAMES F. KING, M.D.
Canton, OH   Timken Mercy Hospital

UNTIED SHOELACES

To the Editor:

Data that I have recently collected at schoolyards and on commuter trains indicate that there is likely to be an epidemic this year of untied shoelaces. Although I originally hypothesized that this problem was limited to teenagers, I must now report that my 8½-year-old son and many of his classmates have succumbed.

Some of the public health consequences of this disease are obvious, such as an increased incidence of falls. However, investigations should begin immediately into the problems of clenched toe, a common strategy to keep untied sneakers on the feet, and bowlegged walking, a strategy to avoid tripping over one's laces.

Meanwhile, health professionals should consider a number of options, including legislation and education. First of all, a bill should be enacted by state legislatures to prohibit untied shoelaces. A stronger solution might be the banning of tie shoes for persons under 21 years of age.

This would have the additional benefit of relieving parents of the burden of teaching their children the skill of tying laces.

A second strategy is to use the talents of health educators. Perhaps advertising campaigns featuring television and recording stars demonstrating the satisfaction one gets from tying one's laces and untying them at the appropriate time would do the trick.

Finally, more research is needed. Foundations must come forth and fund projects on shoestrings. Not to act vigorously is to take the risk of allowing an entire generation to flip-flop in their own footsteps.

SETH B. GOLDSMITH, SC.D.
University of Massachusetts
Amherst, MA   School of Public Health

PUMPKIN CARVER'S PALM

To the Editor:

. . . Pumpkin carver's palm is an affliction of early childhood, but may occur in lighthearted persons of any age. It has a unique seasonal distribution, occurring almost exclusively during the last fortnight in October. It may occur slightly later in the indigent population. The lesion is usually a linear laceration of the palm or thenar eminence, but may also affect the fingers. I have noted lesions of various severity, ranging from superficial wounds, to puncture wounds, to deep and extensive lacerations, with or without tendon involvement.

Though I have not collected enough cases for statistical analysis, I should expect the lesion to occur approximately 93 per cent in the left hand and 7 per cent in the right. The lesion is usually inflicted upon the nondominant hand by the dominant hand, with the aid of a kitchen knife, carving knife, a boy-scout knife or any other suitable carving tool. Men and women are equally affected. Suturing is usually curative and prevention is the key.

I wish to state that the incidence of this affliction is actually very low, so far as the number of people actually at risk is concerned, and do not mean to discourage the practice of pumpkin carving. My worst fear in reporting this malady is that some state legislator somewhere will introduce a bill outlawing pumpkin carving because of its potential hazard to children.

JOEL M. GEIDERMAN, M.D.
Evanston, IL   Evanston Hospital

JEANS FOLLICULITIS

To the Editor:

I have recently seen six cases of what has to be called jeans folliculitis. It is folliculitis of the buttocks, groin, and thighs (usually anterior) caused by ultratight jeans. Patients work in jeans, dance in them, and most recently, jog in them. No other predisposing conditions have been discovered in this small study. Further cases of this disorder may well be seen in younger patients, in view of the rash of advertisements aimed at children.

BRUCE H. HECKMAN, M.D., M.P.H.
Ossining, NY

CHROMOSOME SANS CULOTTE

To the Editor:

. . . How to tell the sex of a chromosome. Just pull down its genes!

MACDONALD WOOD, M.D.

Phoenix, AZ

5

THE ANIMAL KINGDOM
It's Reigning Cats and Dogs, et al.

The human animal shares the planet with other creatures. While some people spurn the association, many cherish it and enthusiastically welcome animals into their lives as pets. Having a pet as a live-in comforts them. Transformed by the magic of human affection, critters with fur, feathers, scales, and shells, critters that walk on all fours as well as those that creep, crawl, and fly, attain the status of personhood as "one of the family."

Bidden or unbidden, however, creature relationships are a fact of life. Indeed, the connection is underscored by a common euphemism for the facts of life: the story of the birds and the bees. Also, we speak of "monkeying" around, and "craning" to see. We're "busy as a bee" and come home "dog-tired" to enjoy a "whale" of a good time, unless a "cat burglar" has taken off like "a bat out of hell" with our "nest egg." In new situations, we feel like "a fish out of water" so we progress at a "snail's pace."

Fortunately, correspondence to the Journal *is just "ducky," even yielding an occasional "horse laugh."*

DOG-WALKER'S ELBOW

To the Editor:

... This summer and fall I had a rather stubborn lateral epicondylitis of my left elbow, and in turn a medial epicondylitis of my right elbow. A rare game of tennis played right-handed (although perhaps not too handily) did not seem likely to be the cause, nor did leaf raking (too early for this) or wood chopping (my son had attended to the wood pile).

Ah! Then it came to me! My black Labrador, Hogan, had a cumulative GPA of about 1.1 in obedience school. Since I had undergone extensive neck surgery in the spring, we increased considerably the amount of time that we walk together. Hogan's residual training causes him to walk on my left side, but he tugs constantly to sniff most bushes, poles, trash containers, fireplugs, and dogs both male and female. Cats and squirrels in particular increase the catecholamine release and thus the traction on my arms.

I usually hold his leash in my left hand with my forearm pronated and the arm extended about 150 degrees. When my left arm became sore, I shifted the leash to my right hand.... To paraphrase Pogo, "We found the enemy, Hogan, and it was us."

Several solutions suggested themselves: stop walking the dog—an option unacceptable to both of us; recycle Hogan through obedience school—perhaps not a bad idea, but he objected; or get a longer leash and assume a "get tough" attitude on my part through firmer commands. This is what we have done, and now my wife walks with us and handles his lead—let him pull *her* epicondyles a bit. Hogan is happy, my arms are better, and all three of us enjoy being out together.

We call the condition "Hogan's elbow," but let us not

add another eponym to the medical literature. Dog-walker's elbow, I expect, would be more widely accept-able.

WILLIAM N. MEBANE, III, M.D.
Philadelphia, PA   Chestnut Hill Hospital

FELINE ACUPUNCTURE

To the Editor:

The perceptive biology watcher, Dr. Lewis Thomas, in his essay "The Long Habit" ... refers to a historic account of the tranquility of imminent death. He mentions a 19th-century memoir about an African explorer who, seized by a lion, experienced an extraordinary sense of peace, calm and painlessness. Dr. Thomas probably knows that the subject of that feline acupuncture was Dr. David Livingstone.

Dr. Livingstone, born in Ulva, Scotland, in 1813, first went to South Africa in 1840 as a medical missionary. In 1843, in what is now Basutoland, he went out with the local people to drive off lions that were molesting the cattle. The native spearmen were soon routed. Livingstone fired at one lion with his muzzle loader and wounded him. While he was reloading, the lion leaped upon Livingstone.

> ... he caught my shoulder as he sprang, and we came to the ground below together. Growling horribly close to my ear, he shook me as a terrier-dog does a rat. The shock produced a stupor similar to that which seems to be felt by a mouse after the first shake of the cat. It caused a sort of dreaminess in which there was no sense of pain nor feeling of terror, though quite conscious of all that was happening. It was like what patients partially under the influence of chloroform describe, who see all the operation, but feel not the knife.... The

shake annihilated fear, and allowed no sense of horror in looking round at the beast. This peculiar state is probably produced in all animals killed by the carnivora, and, if so, is a merciful provision by our benevolent Creator for lessening the pain of death.

The episode ended when the lion released Livingstone and attacked his companion, before dying of the original bullets. Livingstone was left with flesh wounds and a fracture of his left humerus that failed to reunite. This injury was used to identify his remains 31 years later in London. Sir William Fergusson, representing the Royal Geographic Society, described his examination in the *Lancet:*

> Exactly in the region of the attachment of the deltoid to the humerus, there were indications of an oblique fracture. On moving the arm there were the indications of the ununited fracture. A closer investigation and dissection displayed the false joint which had long ago been so well recognized by those who had examined the arm. . . .

Dr. Livingstone, Dr. Thomas and the Chinese acupuncturists may have been observing one characteristic feature of dying, the "most ancient and fundamental of biological functions."

GEORGE V. MANN, M.D.
Vanderbilt University
Nashville, TN   School of Medicine

DANGER ON THE LOS ANGELES FREEWAY

To the Editor:

Hymenoptera stings in the mouth and throat are uncommon but considered dangerous because of possible airway obstruction from local swelling. We treated a patient who was stung in this unusual location while riding his motor-cycle on a Los Angeles freeway.

The patient was a 22-year-old man in excellent health. While he was riding his motorcycle...a stinging insect, probably a bee, flew into his mouth, lodging its stinger in his soft palate. The patient was wearing a helmet but with the visor up. Approximately one hour and 15 minutes later, after completing his journey, the patient removed the stinger and began noticing swelling and pain in the back of his throat. Shortly thereafter, he went to an emergency room and reported shortness of breath and pain and swell-ing in his throat. His pulse was 92, respiratory rate 20, and blood pressure 150/74. Swelling of the uvula and soft pal-ate was noted, as was a small puncture site, presumably caused by the stinger. Over the ensuing three hours, pro-gressive swelling of the pharynx and mouth occurred, re-quiring nasotrachael intubation and treatment....The patient had an uneventful recovery....

The oropharynx is an uncommon site for insect stings. As in the case of our patient, these stings may be severe, requiring close observation and maintenance of an airway. The aggressive drug therapy our patient received may have contributed to his excellent recovery and should be consid-ered in the management of such cases.

Most patients who are stung in the throat probably ac-quire the sting by injesting something on which a bee or wasp has alighted. Our patient was stung in a rather un-usual manner. Had the visor of his helmet been down, his throat would undoubtedly have been protected from the in-sect. We recommend that motorcyclists close visors, or at the very least, keep their mouths closed while riding.

DONALD N. FORTHAL, M.D.
CHRIS LEONG, M.D.
GARY OVERTURF, M.D.
Los Angeles County–University of
Los Angeles, CA   Southern California Medical Center

HOW DOTH THE LITTLE BUSY BEE?

To the Editor:

A "bee sting of the esophagus," as recently reported, must be a rare occurrence.

In 1973, a man was brought to the emergency room with inspiratory stridor and generalized urticaria. He had been drinking beer and playing softball, and he had a history of bee-sting allergy. During treatment, he vomited. The enesis contained a yellow jacket. At about the same time, his friends arrived with the bottle of beer that he had been drinking; it contained several drowned yellow jackets near the bottom.

I believe that this was a case of anaphylaxis resulting from a sting in the esophagus or stomach.

RICHARD P. HANDLER, M.D.
Saranac Lake, NY   Medical Associates of Saranac Lake

To the Editor:

May I be one of many apiarists writing to you in anything but melliferous terms who have been stung by the letter by Farivar . . . in which yellow jackets are promoted to the family of bees? Although both bees and yellow jackets are of the order Hymenoptera, the critter described in the *Journal* belongs to the wasp family (Vespidae)—not the family Apidae.

JOHN B. HAMBLET, M.D.
Cincinnati, OH

AURAL PROPHYLAXIS

To the Editor:

Do not wash the plastic ear pieces of your stethoscope

with fragrant, floral-scented soaps. If you do, bees will fly in your ears looking for honey.

ALBERT E. WARRENS, M.D.

Chico, CA

POLISHING OFF TICKS

To the Editor:

I would like to report a simple and successful method of removing an embedded tick from the skin. This method was suggested to me by my daughter, a 10th-grade student. It was applied successfully on two occasions involving other members of my family, during a recent visit to Cape Cod, Massachusetts.

Approximately two drops of clear fingernail polish are allowed to fall from the brush and completely cover the tick. Within seconds the tick will release its bite and back out of the wound. The tick can then be easily wiped from the skin and properly disposed of.

WARREN T. SHERMAN, M.D.
Danbury, CT   Associated Internists of Danbury

OF LICE AND MEN

To the Editor:

A 47-year-old divorced man was seen because of pubic pruritus. Examination disclosed thickened areas along some of the pubic hair that on microscopical examination appeared to be eggs of the crab louse, *Phthiris pubis*. The patient was advised about the cause of the pruritus. He vehemently denied having had any sexual intercourse for over a year, and the manner in which he acquired the infestation remained a mystery. He was treated with a shampoo containing gamma benzene hexachloride (Kwell shampoo) and improved.

He returned several weeks later for his comprehensive examination and stated that he had given a great deal of thought to what he had been doing during his daily activities to try to explain to himself the manner in which he might have acquired the louse infestation. He managed a men's clothing store selling shorts and trousers. Because the materials and models of the trousers he sold were intriguing in color and very modern, he tried on most of the trousers in his store, some of which undoubtedly had been tried on by many customers. Although *P. pubis* cannot survive for more than 10 to 12 hours apart from a host, the man described could well have acquired the pubic lice from one of his customers.

There is a possibility, then, of acquiring this undesirable itch when one is trying on a new pair of trousers. There is no current method of adequate prevention.

ARMAND MANDEL, M.D.

Parma, OH

GENETIC (VAR.) ALLERGY

To the Editor:

In this fascinating era of rapid changes physicians practicing in exotic climes, as Harvard Square, must remain abreast of a staggering array of local phenomena. They may include mushroom toxicity in patients taking chloroquine; allergic reactions to fire sponges indigenous to Bermuda, hives while preparing edible jelly fish and even a rare fungous infection, tinea nigra palmaris, affecting the sole. This communication is a warning to local practitioners of a new hazard: allergic reactions to an arboreal creature, the genet.

A female mathematician in her twenties was referred to me because of severe allergic symptoms after contact with a shedding genet. The patient was in good health although she had hay fever in the past. She was living uneventfully with two boa constrictors, a few pythons, a gecko, a colony of mice, a rat or two and a domesticated skunk. The genet had been used in a study and had been cared for by several scientists and their families. However, it is a difficult creature to maintain. It dislikes being held and prefers to run free. The creature was given free rein of a bedroom and apparently entered the bed, shedding some hair on the sheets. When the patient entered the bed that night immediate itching and wheezing developed. Further attacks followed exposure only to the genet, which was shedding hair over the house. She obtained relief by spending the night in other quarters. Antihistamines helped only slightly.

Three friends sensitive to cat hair also had asthmatic attacks upon contact with the genet. The patient points out that the creature is not a feline although it is depicted in ancient Egyptian murals as the "family cat." Its musk has been used for perfume.

The Encyclopaedia Britannica lists the genet as any of the catlike creatures, belonging to the genus genetta and the family viverridae, combining the features of a weasel and a cat. Although it is found in southern Europe and its main habitat is in Africa. It is white with black spots and sports a 20 inch, ringed tail.

Those whose allergies relate to the genet (i.e., "genetic") should consider the more hypoallergenic gecko as a pet.

HOWARD S. YAFFEE, M.D.

Cambridge, MA

MORE ON PET-ASSOCIATED ILLNESS

To the Editor:

Our father showed us the article (Oct. 17 issue) and letters (April 17 issue) about all the diseases we can get from cats and dogs. We are nine-year-old brothers, who have Jod Basedow (dog) and Bozo (cat). And we have never had any diseases except chickenpox. We will never give up the Base or Bozo.

BRIAN AND DAVID COREY

San Diego, CA

DID YOU EVER SCOPE A DOLPHIN?

To the Editor:

. . . The local veterinarian had called in high excitement to say that the baby dolphin (over 113 kg) at Marineland was believed to have swallowed the earpiece from a pair of eyeglasses that someone had thrown into the tank. There was fear among the trainers of possible stomach perforation or related dangers.

. . . The baby was still nursing, and could not be taken from its mother's side for long. And, . . . because of its extreme sensitivity and the uncertainty of drug-dosage amounts, the crew believed they could not take the chance of using an anesthetic.

. . . We rushed to our local hospital, picked up Sam's endoscopic equipment and raced to Marineland, where we were met by a group of strong-looking, bronzed young marine biologists. . . . The final strategy that had been agreed upon: they would drain the tank down to a minimum depth of water, leaving just enough for the resident group of dolphins to continue to swim about; into one corner of the tank they would lower a wooden table to hold Sam's equipment plus a V-shaped trestle affair with sponge-rubber pads on the sides to hold the baby dolphin (essentially, they would rig up an "in-tank" operating room); to keep Sam from being electrocuted after plugging in his endoscope, they would put his equipment in extra-strength garbage bags and assign a man to see that things were kept dry (also, they had a wooden block of some sort for the mouth of the dolphin in hopes of avoiding a bitten arm or chewed-up scope—we were deeply grateful for these thoughtful precautions); and, finally, with nets, the crew would carefully ease the baby away from its mother, . . . get it to the trestle and wet-towel it during the procedure. Sam, having climbed down into the tank, would be waiting in his "operating room" to scope his patient as quickly as possible.

So, picture the scene, if you will. Security people have cleared the tank area of visitors. People are excited and curious and craning to see what's going on. Sam, shirtless, wearing borrowed, up-to-the-thigh rubber boots and surgical gloves stands in shallow water at the bottom of the tank preparing to pass his scope into the baby's stomach, while a group of adult dolphins swim around and round corraled off by Jacques-Cousteau-type fellows in brightly colored wet suits. From time to time the baby is patted and sponge-toweled, and emits gentle whistle-squeaks.

Sam is in and out in what seems like only minutes, and, unbelievably, he has extracted the offending earpiece! Triumphantly, he holds it high for all to see, and everyone applauds and laughs with relief. The baby slips smoothly out of the trestle, and heads immediately for its mother's side.

MOLLIE Z. WIRTSCHAFTER

San Pedro, CA

GALLOP—OR CANTER RHYTHM?

To the Editor:

It has recently occurred to me that the term "gallop rhythm" is more often than not a misnomer. It is in the interest of accuracy that the following discussion regarding this term is submitted.

As all knowledgeable horse persons know, when a horse "gallops" each leg strikes the ground individually, producing four distinct beats. A cardiac rhythm containing both an S_3 and an S_4 "gallop" in which there are only three sounds should, in reality, be termed a "canter rhythm," the canter being the gait in which one pair of the horse's diagonal legs strike the ground, simultaneously producing a cadence of three.

CARL N. STEEG, M.D.
New York, NY   Columbia–Presbyterian Medical Center

GALLOP RHYTHMS AND OTHER EQUESTRIAN PROBLEMS

To the Editor:

I note with interest the letter from Carl N. Steeg, M.D. The equestrian information given is correct, but his suggestion to use the term "canter rhythm" would only lead to even more confusion.

Some of our continental colleagues do not use a specific word for canter, but refer to petit galop (France), medio galope (Spain), and piccolo galoppo (Italy), to name but a few.

Since much of the medical literature has a world wide circulation, we might become involved with a piccolo galoppo rhythm! Perhaps we should evolve a more accurate medical terminology.

B. J. DENIS
Slough, England   Johnson & Johnson, Ltd.

SERPENTS TWO WILL NOT DO

To the Editor:

. . . I refer to the description of the *Journal*'s seal as bearing a crossed quill and caduceus. There is indeed a quill, but the staff with a snake twined around it crossing the quill is, in fact, the staff of Asclepius, not the caduceus. Checking my mythology, I find that the caduceus is a staff with two snakes curled around it and two wings at the top, a more elaborate symbol than that which adorns the *Journal*'s cover.

It might be added that the staff of Asclepius is the only true symbol of medicine, since its owner was the Greek god of medicine and healing. The caduceus, on the other hand, was carried by Hermes, the messenger of the Greek gods—an admirable figure, no doubt, but one unconnected with the healing arts. Thus, . . . we may rest assured that the seal of the *Journal* does bear the appropriate emblem.

CHRISTOPHER M. FILLEY
Johns Hopkins University
Baltimore, MD   School of Medicine

BIRDS ON THE MARKET

To the Editor:

Among patients admitted to the New York Neurological

Institute in 1967, with cryptococcal meningitis, two have been employees of New York financial houses.

It has been said that there are too many pigeons on Wall Street.

PAUL L. RICHTER, M.D.
Second Year Resident
New York, NY   New York Neurological Institute

REAL PAIN

To the Editor:

. . . Dr. Spiro writes that it is a burden for the physician "to describe which pain is real and which imaginary." In fact, this decision can be arrived at quite simply: pain occurring in unicorns, griffins and jabberwockies is always imaginary pain, since these are imaginary animals; patients, on the other hand are real, and so they always have real pain. . . .

JOSEPH D. SAPIRA, M.D.
Mobile, AL   University of South Alabama

VALENTINE'S DAY:
IS LOVE REALLY A ZOONOSIS?

To the Editor:

Valentine's Day is a celebration of love dating back to the third century A.D., when the Christian festival of St. Valentine, celebrated on the 14th of February, was fortuitously merged with the pagan ritual of Lupercalia, traditionally celebrated on February 15th. Legend has it that St.

Valentine was known as a benefactor of troubled lovers. Lupercalia was an ancient Roman ceremony with the unromantic goals of ensuring fertility, purifying women, and expiating evil, symbolized by the wolf. All this was accomplished by sacrificing goats and a dog; after that young men, the Luperci, dressed only in goat-skin bikinis, ran among the audience light-heartedly flogging the citizens with thongs made from the same skins. The modern practice of towel snapping clearly derives from the pagan rite, probably with little change in intent.

Since that early time, poets and philosophers have led us all to accept the idea that love is a sickness. But was it always? Certainly not! As Ambrose Bierce observed, the "disease, like caries and other ailments, is prevalent only among civilized races." St. Valentine's Day celebrates that time of transition, from primitive to cultured. But what was the nature of the original malady that is now tradition-fixed and only expressed psychosomatically? For nearly 2000 years, poets and lyricists have faithfully recorded its clinical symptoms: weakness, aching, malaise, insomnia, recurrent depression, a rise in evening temperature, and sometimes even heartbreak. Any second-year medical student worthy of a learner's caduceus would tell you that these symptoms are characteristic of brucellosis. History tells the rest. *Brucella meltitensis* is an infection of goats transmissible to human beings by contact, as in the Lupercalian rite of flogging with skins of freshly killed animals. Indeed, the etiologic agent was finally discovered in goats on the Mediterranean island of Malta late in the 19th century. Obviously, the heathens had perpetuated a zoonosis and innocently elevated it to epidemic status by their well-intentioned custom. With the Christianization of Lupercali, the whole thing got mixed together and entered our folklore and consciousness. Even the now popular belly dance symbolizes the undulant character of the love-linked infection.

Oh, how chancy life is! Just imagine what our literature, lyrics, and even love itself would be like if those old goats had had anthrax!

A. L. RITTERSON, PH.D.
Rochester, NY   University of Rochester Medical Center

6

OCCUPATIONAL INJURIES
Work Can Be Hazardous to Your Health

Employment application forms should carry a warning label: Work Can Be Hazardous to Your Health. This notice is not meant to deter participants, only to alert workers to dangerous side effects, including addiction. Workaholics are phobic, fearing that even a lunch break may fracture advancement opportunities. But pulling oneself up by the bootstraps can strain more than the back. In some cases, the payoff is as likely to be an injury as a paycheck.

No doubt about it, earning a living is risky business. Obvious perils abound in certain occupations—astronaut, steeplejack, miner, race-car driver. Less often recognized are the boobytraps in mundane careers. Yet, doctors' files bulge with case histories, evidence that any workplace can jeopardize well-being.

Jobholders beware! Even a desk job, reading books, is not without hazards. A California physician treated a patient with just such a job and a work-related injury that the Journal *promptly dubbed "proofreader's prostatitis."*

PROOFREADER'S PROSTATITIS

To the Editor:

   ... The patient, a divorced, 38-year-old man, has been employed as a printer and proofreader for most of his adult life. His past history is relatively uneventful. . . .

On February 13, 1969, he presented himself with symptoms of urinary frequency and seminal discharge of two weeks' duration. The discharge was described as "resembling that which follows sexual intercourse." Examination of the prostate showed it to be about twice the normal size, extremely boggy and extremely tender. . . . The syndrome began during the time the patient was continuously occupied with proofreading what is often termed "salacious literature." As the patient put it, "I was always turned on. . . ."

The prostatis was given conventional treatment, and recovery was uneventful except for one relapse after what was described as a "wild weekend."

My problem is whether to consider the illness to be an industrial accident or to ascribe it to personal hypersensitivity to an exciting stimulus.

MAURICE L. KAMINS, M.D.

Los Angeles, CA

LADDER SHINS

To the Editor: A 52-year-old man presented to me for evaluation of back pain. . . . The physical examination was essentially unremarkable except for two 1.5-cm hard nodules symmetrically over the mid-tibial area . . . A detailed history revealed that these nodules had been present over the past 10 years, more or less waxing and waning. He attributed the swelling to his occupation (installing automatic garage-door openers), in which he constantly stood on a ladder. The right leg had slightly larger swelling since he leaned more heavily on the right extremity. Several years later, after several bouts of cellulitis and infection in these areas, he found the solution; carpeting the ladder steps. This approach lessened the irritation and prevented infection. Interestingly enough, his 14-year-old son began having the same lesions when he joined hs father's occupation.

I asked the patient what he thought the lesions were. The answer came instantly: "ladder shins," as if it were a well-recognized occupational disease.... In all honesty, I didn't know that the disease "ladder shins" ever existed; I searched all over the literatuare and asked everyone I knew in the next few weeks, and finally gave up. I thought the patient's own description was good enough. I could call it "Rao's syndrome," but again, why another eponym?

D. SUDHAKER RAO, M.D.
Detroit, MI   Henry Ford Hospital

PRICER PALSY

To the Editor:

A right-handed grocery-store clerk was referred for electromyography and nerve-conduction studies to evaluate a report of numbness in the ulnar side of her left hand that had been present for about two months. She had also noted an occasional aching discomfort in the area. There was a definite exacerbation of the symptoms when she was at work, running the "UPC" pricing code on food items over the code-sensing machine at the checkout counter.... A small area of decreased sensation was noted on the dorsum of the left hand in the area between the fourth and fifth metacarpals. . . .

After the operation the patient had a return of sensation in the area of numbness, except for a small, 0.5-mm area distally. Three months after the neurolysis, repeated electrodiagnostic studies documented nearly complete improvement in both the distal latency and amplitude.

This case documents a "pricer palsy." . . . The way the patient ran the food items over the code-sensing machine involved very fast, repetitive pronation, with marked wrist flexion. . . . In view of the markedly increased use of price-code sensors in retail sales, there should be consideration of pricer palsy in clerks presenting with numbness and aching in the hard dorsum.

JACQUELINE J. WERTSCH, M.D.

Milwaukee, WI   The Medical College of Wisconsin

TOBACCO-PRIMER'S WRIST

To the Editor:

. . . I would like to call attention to an occupational hazard not previously described yet commonly seen in the "tobacco belt."

A healthy 17-year-old recently presented with an area of pain and swelling localized over the origin of the tendons of the abductor policis longus and extensor policis brevis where they overlie the tendons of the extensor carpi radialis longus and brevis. . . . In the previous week the patient had been employed to prime tobacco. This task requires repeated movement of the arm with pronation in association with extension and abduction of the thumb . . . followed by forceful and rapid flexion and adduction of the thumb to prune the tobacco leaves manually from the stalk.

The customary home remedies of liniment and soaking with Epsom salt (hydrated magnesium sulfate) provided little relief for this "tobacco-primer's wrist." Local infiltration with a depot steroid and splinting aided in recovery . . . over a period of several days.

JAMES S. PARSONS, M.D.
Raleigh, NC

PIPETTER'S THUMB

To the Editor:

. . . A 53-year-old man was referred to the hospital because of a tremor of six months duration. There was a coarse, irregular tremor of the upper extremities, more marked distally and on voluntary movements; the neurologic examination was otherwise normal. The patient was a laboratory-glassware manufacturer, and he used to gauge his pipettes with mercury; he would frequently lick off his right thumb, which occluded the pipette, because, he said, it helped to keep a mercury-proof seal. Pipettes were only part of his production; nevertheless, he had gauged at least 1000 pipettes per month for more than 30 years. His urinary mercury levels were high, and since other causes of tremor were excluded, inorganic mercury poisoning was diagnosed. No other source of contamination was detected; the tremor eventually disappeared after cessation of exposure and dimercaprol treatment.

Minuk et al. recently reported on one of the pipetter's specific diseases; we must keep in mind that a pipetter's thumbs may be involved in other diseases as well.

E. ROULLET, M.D.
P. CASTAIGNE, M.D.
Paris, France   Hospital de la Salpetrière

POSTER PRESENTER'S THUMB

To the Editor:

Presentations at national meetings can bring prestige and peril. The hazards of slide presentations include recalcitrant audiovisual equipment and obnoxious skeptics. Anxiety attacks and wounded egos are common. Physical injury is rare. Poster presentations decrease some psychological and technical risks but pose a unique hazard.

A 38-year-old right-handed man used 80 Push Pins (Douglas Stewart Co., Madison, WI) to mount his scientific presentation on a standard, unreceptive, 1.2-by-2.4-mm poster board. On completion of the task, the patient noted painful erythema on the volar aspect of his right thumb. In 15 minutes, a 6-by-7-mm blister appeared; it ruptured during the subsequent dismantling of the poster. The patient recalled similar trauma associated with his use of standard thumb tacks at previous meetings. A poll of other poster presenters revealed numerous similar unpublished cases. Prolific patients had multiple recurrences.

Considering the widespread use of poster sessions, thousands of similar cases must occur annually. Organizations that invite such sessions should provide user-friendly boards to reduce the incidence of "poster presenter's thumb."

LAUREL C. PREHEIM, M.D.
Creighton University
Omaha, NE   School of Medicine

WAITER'S SHOULDER

To the Editor:

A 52-year-old woman who had been working as a waitress for 20 years presented herself in our arthritis clinic with severe pain on abduction and extension of the left shoulder. She stated that she could no longer carry heavy trays in the classic underhand, shoulder-high position.

On examination of the shoulder point, tenderness was found. . . . She was treated . . . and improved in four days. She returned to work carrying heavy dinner trays on the fifth day, only to relapse within 24 hours. . . . She was again treated. . . .

May we, therefore, add the euphonious eponym "waiter's shoulder" to the growing literature on occupational bursitis? We apologize to the equal, but fair sex, for what is perhaps our chauvinist bias in rejecting as unwieldy, the alternative "waitress's bursitis."

DAVID A. BENNAHUM, M.D.
WILLIAM WILLIAMS, M.D.
University of New Mexico
Albuquerque, NM   School of Medicine

GENU GENUFLECTORUM REVISITED

To the Editor:

Dr. Bracken . . . has been criticized by "Minerva" of the *British Medical Journal* for coining the term "genu genuflectorum" when the Anglo-Saxon "clergyman's knee" has long been a term for infrapatellar bursitis. "Minerva" is unjust. Dr. Bracken's letter describes a priest with an effusion of noninflammatory fluid in the left knee. The diagnosis is quite correctly given as chronic lateral meniscus stress rather than a bursitis (clergyman's or housemaid's) in which the fluid would naturally contain inflammatory cells.

However, I must protest that genuflection on the left knee seems an unusual liturgical practice. My ecclesiastical adviser (a Benedictine monk and former Royal Navy officer) informs me that an attempt at genuflection on the left knee while one was wearing a sword would be fraught with danger. He also draws my attention to the earliest description of clergyman's knee, by Hegesippus (second century) in his *Life of the Apostle St. James the Less:* "His knees became hard like a camel's for he was continually bending the knee in worship to God." Even this case of asceticism pales beside that of the 12th-century Ethiopian hermit St. Tekla Haymanot. His austerity led to the loss of a foot, for which the Lord compensated him by giving him three pairs of wings—a case, surely, of alae neoplasticae secondary to eremetic gangrene.

WILLIAM E. GRIFFITHS, M. A., B.M., B.C.
Plymouth, England   Plymouth General Hospital

GAMBA LEG

To the Editor:

The 1981 Boston Early Music Festival evoked considerable interest in early music and musical instruments. The treble viola da gamba is an early small string instrument somewhat larger than a violin . . . gripped firmly between the knees for playing.

A 38-year-old woman reported numbness and paresthesia along the medial aspect of the left leg distal to the knee, in the distribution of the cutaneous branches of the saphenous nerve. The cause defied explanation until she noted that she had begun practicing the treble viola da gamba only two months before. Because of fear of dropping the instrument, considering its newness and cost, she was gripping it between her knees with nearly teeth-clenching rigor. . . . She had been inflicting almost daily trauma to the nerve for nearly two months.

After placing a soft sponge or cloth pad between her knees and the instrument, the symptoms rapidly disappeared, and she is now entirely cured. Playing with more confidence, she no longer grips the instrument so tightly. I have called the syndrome "gamba leg" (with apologies to experts in Italian). . . .

PHILLIP L. HOWARD, M.D.
Burlington, VT   University of Vermont

GAMBA GAMBA

To the Editor:

I trust that Dr. Howard . . . is aware that viola da gamba means leg viola, and so, "leg viola leg."

MILFORD D. SCHULZ, M.D.
Boston, MA   Massachusetts General Hospital

STRESSED MUSICIANS

To the Editor:

. . . A few years ago I had the opportunity to telemeter electrocardiograms from professional singers, symphony musicians and conductors during actual public performances and observed the frequent occurrence of arrhythmias, including marked tachycardias and, in certain wind players, dramatic Valsalva-like responses. Since physicians may encounter musicians as patients I consider it important for them to be aware of these stresses. Whether or not such stresses are ever harmful seems an individual matter but one that should be considered if the cardiovascular status of a patient is ever in question.

Too often, music making is considered a benign labor of love. It may be, but to the professional it can also be very hard work. For instance, I saw conductors maintain an average increase in heart rate of 89 percent during performances. The belief that most conductors invariably live to ripe old ages just is not so. The average life-span of the 112 conductors indexed in Schonberg's *The Great Conductors* who have died within this century from noncatastrophic causes computes to 71.2 + [or] − 10.1 years—a respectable but hardly remarkable figure.

A study by Tucker et al. notes that the life expectancy of musicians is 22 per cent under the national average and that coronary disease accounts for almost 5 per cent more deaths than in the general population. These statistics are more sober than might be appreciated at first glance.

STANLEY D. DAVIS, PH.D.
San Francisco, CA

MUSICAL MEDICINE

To the Editor:

The purpose of this letter is to ask that the profession treat musicians of all ages with respect for their artistic sensitivities and to realize fully the importance of their dependence upon hands, limbs, mouth, ears, etc.

It is suggested that "interested" physicians across the

nation . . . set up a network for musical referral. Thus, when a cellist from the Boston Symphony is afflicted in Dallas, he can have access to someone who understands his peculiar needs, and who might even monitor the evening performance.

. . . Any imaginative physician can visualize the impact of otherwise common lesions when applied to a practicing musician.

Lesions such as "tennis elbow" in a bowing arm, an axillary abscess, a paronychia or a developing Dupuytren contracture are all perilous to the string section. For the brass and woodwind, a stutter that develops under stress, a smashed lip (the result of a mugging), an asthmatic attack, an inguinal hernia, a nasty "cold sore," and infected in-growing hairs on the upper lip all seriously compromise the eight-hour daily routine of practice before performance.

The finger pads of a flutist or the callus of a harpist or guitarist become torn and infected too easily, and the pianist practicing for eight hours with a maladjusted pedal can end up crippled for the evening concert. All keyboard performers who suffer fracture dislocations of their fingers will recover "full function" in the normal sense, but the ability to perform a regular trill once again demands an associated "musical physical-therapy" approach. A small decrease in hearing ability from an otitis media or a seeing disability from a contact-lens conjunctivitis can be crucial at a prize-winning contest.

The more "elective" problems can be represented by a hasty tonsillectomy, which will change a vocalist's resonating chamber and will require skilled follow-up speech therapy. Similarly, the unthinking insertion of intravenous needles into the backs of hands and feet in these patients must be guarded against. A ganglion of an organist's wrist and unsightly facial and other nervi require the services of skilled plastic surgeons with special interest in these areas.

The esthetic consideration is related to the correction of severe scolioses, deformed limbs, the employment of cosmetic surgery and the skillful use of various prostheses.

JOHN B. DAWSON, M.A., F.R.C.P.
Brookings, SD   South Dakota State University

To the Editor:

...I am a second year medical student, and have had a long and active involvement in music. I have personally experienced such "musical medical" dilemmas as being a trombonist with orthodontic braces, a percussionist with tendonitis in both shoulders, and a pianist with traumatic lower-back pain. Lest I also sound like a fiddler with severe hypochondriasis, I should add that I am frequently, if not usually, in excellent health!...

KAY B. CYNAMON
University of Pennsylvania
Philadelphia, PA   Medical Center

WIND PAROTITIS

To the Editor:

Recurrent parotitis is considered to be an idiopathic disease. I have encountered 4 patients with this disease, in each of whom the development of the parotitis was preceded by a history of the patient's engaging in blowing a wind instrument such as a trumpet or clarinet. One patient gave a history of having very forcefully blown up some heavy balloons....

HENRY F. SAUNDERS, M.D.
Cleveland, OH

To the Editor:

Dr. Saunders . . . reports on four patients who played wind instruments and in whom "wind parotitis" developed. . . .

Previous reports regarding similar episodes have included musicians, glassblowers, balloon blowers and persons who have consciously developed the trick of causing immediate and repeated parotid swelling by increasing intraoral pressure. Such swellings can hardly be explained on the basis of infection. The time factor of immediate swelling, as well as regression without treatment, would militate against an infectious origin. . . .

LOUIS MANDELL, D.D.S.
Columbia University School
Bronx, NY   of Dental and Oral Surgery

To the Editor:

. . . At the staging area of the French Foreign Legion in North Africa, mumps appeared, and swollen parotids became epidemic, recurring and relapsing. It appeared that men had found that by blowing hard (they used bottles as resistance) they could force air up into the parotids, simulating mumps. Thus, they were in relatively cool hospitals, had cooling drinks, and escaped K.P., guard duty and patrols, and there was difficulty finding adequate rosters of men outside the hospital to maintain necessary duties.

Someone remembered, however, that mumps is a systemic disease, with spinal-fluid pleocytosis. Patients with new cases of swollen parotids therefore received a prompt spinal puncture; unless the cell count was up, the yard birds got 2 C.C.'s and active duty. The frequency of parotitis waned promptly.

ROGER A. HEMPHILL, M.D.
Marion, IN

PENILE VENEREAL EDEMA

To the Editor:

. . . We should like to call attention to an unusual traumatic lesion of the penis that seems to be peculiar to young military personnel and tourists arriving at Bangkok on "rest and recreation (R & R) leave."

A 23-year-old soldier appeared at the hospital during the morning after his arrival at Bangkok for "rest and recreation" from duty in Vietnam. He complained of a sore penis, which he had noted that morning. For about 1 year he had been stationed in Vietnam, where, owing to the isolation of his post, he had been sexually abstinent for several months. The evening of his arrival in Thailand he met a "bar girl" and had coitus through the night—a total of some 6 to 8 times. No condoms were used, and his partner "was rather passive." Physical examination revealed a circumcised, anxious man with an edematous area involving approximately 30 per cent of the mucosal surface of the remaining prepuce. . . . The skin was not abraded, the area was not tender, and a urethral smear was unremarkable. A Venereal Disease Research Laboratory test was nonreactive. A diagnosis of "friction injury of the penis" was made, and sexual abstinence for a few days prescribed. The patient, though rather unhappy with the treatment, made an uneventful and rapid recovery.

We have been confronted by this type of penile lesion rather frequently at Bangkok and have seen at least 25 to 30 such patients during the period between 1968 and 1972. The "syndrome" was more common during the peak of Bangkok's popularity as an "R & R Center" and seems to have been limited almost exclusively to young, vigorous personnel who came with great expectations from isolated locations in Vietnam. . . . It appears to be more common in circumcised men. A "hardened" and sexually nonparticipating partner with little vulval mucous secretion seems to be part of the background in every case. The penile lesion often baffles the novice medical officer. The diagnosis is based on the history, lack of an incubation period, characteristic physical appearance and absence of paraphimosis. . . . Rapid recovery occurs with rest of the injured appendage. . . .

JOHN P. CANBY, M.D.
HENRY WILDE, M.D.
APO San Francisco, CA   U.S. Army Hospital

A CASE OF CHRONIC DENIAL

To the Editor:

The syndrome of "chronic denial" should be called to the attention of all university-affiliated physicians and personnel. The course of the affliction runs rampant through medical-school classes, as most students undoubtedly know, but to my knowledge has never been adequately described.

Primary symptoms of the chronic-denial student include such trite expressions as "I hardly got anything done in my seven hours of studying last night!" and "I only got to read a few pages of Goodman and Gilman for the test!" and "There's so much to read, I don't know how I'll ever get it done." The afflicted student might surface from the endless mental treks through the human morass on Saturday evening, but only because of peer-group pressure to prove to his or her fellow compatriots that "I don't study all the time!"

Pathognomonic of the "chronic-denial syndrome" is the student who can always be found in the classroom or library studying away the hours and at the same moment informing you of how little he ever accomplishes and how he wishes he were like so-and-so and what he might be doing this weekend.

Complications of this syndrome are primarily manifested in other students. It drives us crazy!

EDWARD J. LYNCH
St. Louis University
St. Louis, MO   School of Medicine

GRAND-ROUNDS WHIPLASH

To the Editor:

I should like to take this opportunity to report what must be a frequent syndrome among the fatigued house staff of our teaching hospitals, and from which I recently suffered. This complex might best be termed "grand-rounds whiplash."

Approximately two weeks ago severe spasm of my cervical muscles developed unilaterally, and was intense enough to prevent my continuing in my hospital duties for several days. There had been no prior similar incident and no known trauma. Routine studies were negative, and no cause was evident. In the following week I dozed off at grand rounds and awoke with a start, rapidly flexing my neck and producing a similar syndrome.

It is my assumption that this type of cervical whiplash injury in the sleepy house officer at grand rounds is probably not an uncommon occurrence. One must wonder whether lecturers at grand rounds need insure themselves against their personal liability for this obvious occupational hazard—or should the house staff be issued prophylactic Thomas collars?

STEPHEN G. PAUKER, M.D.
Fellow in Cardiology
Boston, MA   New England Medical Center Hospitals

GRAND-ROUNDS WHIPLASH: PREDISPOSING CAUSE

To the Editor:

. . . Dr. Pauker raised the question whether the entity "grand-rounds whiplash" was more widespread than heretofore realized. This letter only seems to point out that for all Dr. Pauker's expertise, he failed to follow the time-honored instruction to all in medicine: "Take a careful and complete history."

Review of Dr. Pauker's letter will show that "routine studies were negative." All well and good. His recent history of cervical muscle spasms was interesting but a more complete history would reveal that he had been a medical visitor to the Katahdin region recently and while there had occupied a seat in my aircraft while we toured the mountain and surrounding woodlands. It was *here* that the syndrome actually began. Dr. Pauker, it seems, is a victim of acrophobia and in attempting to "retract himself" in a protective way (as a turtle into a nonexistent shell) strained his cervical muscles and aggravated them later on at Grand Rounds.

Since we all try to learn from all things in medicine the lesson must be that all "acrophobic fellows" should not fly with me before going on Grand Rounds. This might be much less expensive than the suggested prophylactic Thomas collars.

H. C. GILMAN, M.D.

Millinocket, ME

AN INTERN'S LOT

To the Editor:

I consider myself a tolerant man, ready to put up with the effusions of the younger generation—but the *Journal* has finally turned me off. Students running our national conventions . . . radicals in our media, our political party, and our congress . . . sex in the classroom, the nursery and the premature ward . . . revolution, pornography, and free love I can take in my stride.

But when the *Journal* prints an article suggesting that interns might need more sleep than they traditionally get, I draw the line. O tempora! O mores!

ALFRED B. MASON, M.D.

Brooklyn, NY

"AN OPEN LETTER TO TODAY'S GENTLEMAN-PHYSICIAN"

To the Editor:

You needn't tip your hat to me,
Nor hold the door as I pass through,
Nor buy my meal when we dine out,
Nor yield your seat when chairs are few.

You needn't compliment my gown,
Nor send me flowers or pretty sweets,
Nor help me don my coat or cape,
Nor take my arm when crossing streets.

You needn't curb your salty tongue,
Nor shield me from a tale risqué.
In fact, you needn't cater to
My gender, sir, in any way.

Such courtly customs I'll forsake
If you'll comply with just this one:
To put back down the toilet seat,
Sir, after micturition's done.

(Written after plunging into the icy depths of a physician's water closet.)

PATRICIA A. LIPSCOMB, M.D., PH.D.
University of Washington
Seattle, WA   School of Medicine

"AN OPEN LETTER TO A LIBERATED LADY PHYSICIAN"

Dear Dr. Lipscomb, you must be
Of Lilliputian ancestry
If you can "plunge" (your word) into
The "icy depths" of one small loo.

I think you meant your fundament
Alone made such a sad descent.
Take care with words or, nymph, you'll find
It chill on more than your behind:

Your letter seven times says "nor"—
Supererogatory for
After a "not" a "nor" doth give
A glaring double negative.

And men should serve your sex, you say,
By dropping toilet seats: that way
And in no other. Ne'er, you meant,
Drop aught besides? Good wench, relent—

Else man's sad epitaph shall read:
"Enthroned in comfort women peed
And had men think on maiden's thighs
Only when doing up their flies."

JOHN S. BRADSHAW, M.B., CH.B.

Galway, Ireland

7

FADS
Giving the Frisbee the Finger

Fads just happen. They emerge spontaneously like Minerva fully grown from the head of Zeus. To be sure, the whole experience probably gave Zeus an ungodly headache and, similarly, recent fads have contributed a body of physical ailments to medical literature. A fad is highly contagious. In the syndrome, the germ of an idea infects a susceptible population, which suffers an immediate and intense reaction, including a fever. In most cases, however, the patient returns to normal when the crisis passes.

Fads mock the cliché that there's nothing new under the sun. Relentless pursuit of the latest in entertainment, fashion, and recreation guarantees innovation. For years people jogged or strolled along sidewalks, some checking out shop windows, others ogling passersby—until one day just about every walker took on the appearance of a robot, glassy-eyed, with a plastic knob plugged into his or her ear. A dangling wire connected the listener to a compact battery-powered radio.

STEREO EARPHONES AND HEARING LOSS

To the Editor:

Since 1979, portable FM radios and stereo cassette players with featherweight earphones have achieved considerable popularity. Routinely, unit volume levels are set by the wearer to override conversation, traffic noise, and other environmental sounds the wearer may wish to block out. These portable units can conveniently be worn for extended periods of time, and since noise-induced hearing loss is a result of intensity (loudness) and duration of exposure, these units may be capable of inducing a hearing loss.

The Occupational Safety and Health Act (OSHA) of 1970 stipulates that hearing-conservation programs be instituted for industry when employees are exposed to sound environments of 85 dB or higher, as measured with a sound-level meter using the A Scale (dB A). Current standards allow a maximum time-weighted daily exposure of 90 dB A for eight hours, 95 dB A for four hours, 100 dB A for two hours, and so on. No exposure to continuous sound above 115 dB A is allowed.

Three randomly chosen stereo units were analyzed by means of a Bruel and Kjaer sound-level meter (Type 4152 and NBS9A coupler). Two portable FM radios and one stereo cassette player playing two different tapes were evaluated. The range of intensity was recorded for each volume setting.... At volume setting 4, the intensity ranged from 93 to 108 dB A. At volume setting 8 and above, the intensity level was predominantly in excess of 115 dB A for all units tested.

In the light of what is known regarding noise and its effect on hearing, there can be no doubt that these units have the potential for inducing a permanent bilateral sensorineural hearing loss—especially if they are used at a volume setting of 4 or above for extended periods.

ARNOLD E. KATZ, M.D.
HUBERT L. GERSTMAN, D.ED.
ROBERT G. SANDERSON, M.A.
ROBERT BUCHANAN, M.S.
Boston, MA　　　　Tufts–New England Medical Center

SPACE-INVADERS WRIST

To the Editor:

. . . Arm chair athletes can now rejoice. I think that I have made a discovery that can add the more sedentary to the sport-related injured.

I had been puzzled by a stiff, painful right wrist that had gradually developed over approximately one month. The rigors of medical school and cold winter weather had combined to prevent any vigorous sporting activities, and I could recall no trauma to the area. There was no soft-tissue change or limitation of range of motion, and the pain was certainly not excruciating. The problem was mainly a nuisance. At radiography the wrist was entirely normal.

In further quest of a reason for my malady, I discovered a probable cause. A friend had recently acquired a video game containing a very popular game cassette (Atari, Space Invaders), which I played quite frequently after its purchase. It can be operated by one or two players and has a hand-held control box with a movable "stick" or "paddle." The paddle is yoked in the center of the box, allowing its motion through 360 degrees, and depending on the particular game cassette, it requires a large number of rapid, repetitive arm movements, including flexion and extension of the wrist and pronation and supination of the forearm, to maneuver a spacecraft to avoid bombs, rockets, or alien attackers. The position of the "fire" button almost necessitates right-handed operation. Other models have a similar basic design.

The symptoms could have been due to minor ligamentous strain of the joint from repeated, prolonged playing. Further use of the game certainly aggravated them, whereas 1½ weeks of abstinence produced noticeable improvement. Another person who is a frequent video-game player has similar, although less pronounced symptoms.

To my knowledge, this is the first reported case of "Space-Invaders wrist," and it may be an important consideration in the diagnosis of unilateral wrist pain in an otherwise healthy video-game player. This case may also warrant investigation of the bio-mechanical design of such games in order to minimize what may be an increasing problem with the growing electronic-game-playing public. My greatest concern is that this letter will prompt a wave of reports of video-game injuries (if not a subspecialty of sports medicine). In view of the booming video-game industry, the possibilities, unfortunately, appear endless: "Asteroids" osteoarthritis, pinball palsy, phaser felon. . . .

TIMOTHY C. McCOWAN
College of Medicine
Little Rock, AR   University of Arkansas

VIDEO-GAME PALSY: DISTAL ULNAR NEUROPATHY IN A VIDEO-GAME ENTHUSIAST

To the Editor:

An occupational paralysis of the muscles supplied by the deep palmar branch of the ulnar nerve was first described in 1896 under the title "A Peculiar Form of Progressive Muscular Atrophy in Gold Polishers." The neuropathic origin was recognized by Hunt in 1908 when he reported distal ulnar neuropathy after prolonged oyster opening. Cases have also followed shoveling with a spade, carpentry, and the use of vibrating buffers, wire cutters, leather-cutting knives, floor polishers, and pneumatic drills. . . . Distal paralysis of the ulnar nerve at the wrist has also been described in motorcyclists and bicyclists. We now report distal ulnar neurapathy in a video-game player.

A 28-year-old man noted loss of feeling in the medial two fingers of the left hand for two months, with weakness of the left hand and callus formation on the base of the left hypothenar eminence. Clawing of these two fingers was also noted, with difficulty in spreading the fingers apart. For one month he had played video games four to six times a day (10-minute duration of each game). While playing the games, he rested the extended left hand on the machine, with pressure on the hypothenar eminence (at the side of the callus), and used the left fingers to turn a rotary knob. He stopped playing the games three weeks before being seen, with improvement of sensory symptoms.

. . . This recreational neuropathy probably resulted from excessive pressure on the deep branch of the ulnar nerve in the extended hand. As expected from the location of the callus, both the deep and superficial branches were affected. . . .

Video games have become a popular form of recreation, but the hazards of this activity have not been well established. Video games may affect subjects with light-sensitive epilepsy, and prolonged playing may cause wrist pain ("space-invaders wrist") or de Quervain's stenosing tenosynovitis. The present case documents a new complication.

ROBERT P. FRIEDLAND, M.D.
JAMES N. ST. JOHN, M.D.
Martinez, CA   Veterans Administration Medical Center

LACK OF INTERPERSONAL COMMUNICATION IN PROGRAMMED LEARNING

To the Editor:

Recently there has been publicity in the press regarding the passage of an ordinance in some communities that would ban young people from playing computer games in galleries designed for that purpose. The reason for this ban, which has been supported by some psychologists, is the fear that this activity has averse effects on the developing young person. It is said that the youngster can become absorbed in these games and conditioned to a form of behavior that isolates him or her from other forms of interpersonal communications. It is feared that this leads to the development of a hostile individual who has difficulty in interacting with others. Although I have no expertise in this field, I find the allegations, if true, ironic. The ultimate extension of the behavioral activity involved in computer games has long been encouraged by professional educators in the form of programmed learning techniques. Although programmed learning is perhaps as effective in communicating facts, the contrast between this form of education and one that encourages the student to interact with others is striking. It seems to me that this must be considered when we adopt computerized educational techniques in our medical curricula. Are we producing a doctor who is at a disadvantage with respect to social intercourse when we encourage an educational system that excludes dependence on interpersonal communications?

EDMUND J. LEWIS, M.D.
Rush-Presbyterian–
Chicago, IL   St. Luke's Medical Center

FRISBEE FINGER

To the Editor:

...We wish to report here an especially-affiliated hazard of the common man's discus—the entity of "Frisbee finger."

A 22-year-old man was seen with pain of the right middle finger. On the day of presentation he gave a history of prolonged use of a Moonlighter Frisbee (Wham-o Mfg. Company, San Gabriel, CA) with a subsequent inability to continue his game because of painful abrasion of the lateral aspect of the proximal phalange of the right middle finger. He stated that this abrasion, with consequent pain, began as a small rubbing sensation experienced on each throw of the Frisbee, with intensity increasing to an unbearable level until continuance of activity was deemed impossible.

Physical examination revealed an alert, oriented, cooperative man with stable vital signs. A tender abrasion, 1.5 cm by 1.0 cm, of the lateral aspect of the right-middle-finger proximal phalange was noted, with a clear, fluid-filled vesicle, 0.5 cm in diameter, located just distal to the abrasion, on the anterolateral aspect of the proximal interphalangeal joint. Coincidentally, a similar vesicle, 0.5 cm in diameter, was found on the posterior aspect of the right thumb.

After the abrasion was treated, the patient was advised to discontinue his Frisbee activity for at least two weeks. Instead, he pursued his avocation and returned on the following day with an abrasion of the same area, now increased in size. Both vesicles were ruptured and soiled.

This case demonstrates the typical findings of what we now call "Frisbee finger": abrasion of the middle finger on the dominant hand, with or without concomitant clear vesicles distal to the abrasion and vesicles on the thumb of the same hand.

Though further inquiry is indicated, cure of this entity can be established currently only by discontinuance of the harmful activity. Bandage protection as an adjunct to healing is to no avail, since the jagged Frisbee edge will either wear away the bandage or become otherwise entangled, placing severe limitations on the accuracy of throw.

We have found that Frisbee finger has a higher rate among city dwellers because constant use of the Frisbee on hard surfaces produces jagged edges, which intensify and facilitate the abrasive action on the middle finger. The syndrome does occur with overuse of smooth-edge Frisbees as well, however, and should not be ruled out in subjects from more rural settings.

HALLEY S. FAUST
MARK L. DEMBERT, M.D.

Philadelphia, PA

To the Editor:

> A Frisbee's fun is not as fabled,
> In fact, you might become disabled
> With bursting blisters on your finger
> You'll fail in feigning as a flinger.
>
> Yes, Frisbee finger now is put
> With tennis elbow, athlete's foot,
> Abuses of athletic action—
> Will someone's tossing thumb need traction?
>
> I do not argue the contention
> Abstention is the best prevention;
> So have it printed on each disk:
> "You toss this plate at your own risk."
>
> No doubt Frisbeers will still flip
> Though "flicted flippers" disks may slip;

Still some will say the cautious course is:
"Don't play around with flying saucers."

BARRY S. LEVY, M.D.

Minnetonka, MN

NOTE: Dr. Franz Ingelfinger, then Journal *editor, couldn't resist concluding the extensive correspondence on Frisbee finger with the following comments.*

JOURNAL NOTE: The Journal *has just received in the mail a new book, called* Frisbee, *which, according to the* Saturday Review, *"should not be tossed aside lightly." Its author is a psychiatrist, Dr. Stancil E.D. Johnson....*

Frisbee *contains a chapter by Roger Woods, M.D., entitled "Medical Aspects of Frisbee."...Frisbee finger, according to Dr. Woods, consists predominantly of injury to the fingernail, which if present in its most serious manifestation ("Grade III") may lead to "avulsion...of the nail from the underlying bed." "Band-Aids" appear preferable to the "adhesive tape" recommended by our correspondents, but for temporary relief Dr. Woods cites others to the effect that the afflicted fingertip be immersed in cold beer.*

Frisbee finger, *Ingel Finger regretfully acknowledges, has not been adequately covered in the pages of the* Journal.—Ed.*

JAWS NEUROSIS

To the Editor:

We wish to report an unusual case of "cinematic neurosis."

A 17-year-old girl was referred to the Neurology Service because of nuchal rigidity, jerking of the limbs and hallucinations of being attacked by sharks.

Three days before admission she had seen the motion picture *Jaws*. Later that evening, after discussing the film with her friends, she became frightened and upset. On the following day she began having episodes of jerking of the limbs, screaming, and partial loss of awareness and was admitted to a hospital, where she was treated. . . . Nuchal rigidity developed and she was transferred to Wichita because of the possibility that she had meningitis with convulsions. She and her family denied any previous psychiatric or neurologic problems.

Clinical examination was within normal limits apart from neck stiffness and a coarse tremor of the outstretched hands. Routine laboratory studies were normal, as were her electroencephalogram and cerebrospinal fluid.

During the next three days she had a total of five episodes of terror in which she repeatedly screamed "sharks, sharks" and jerked her limbs in an irregular and asymmetrical fashion. She did not respond appropriately to verbal stimulation during these episodes, which all occurred in the evenings. At other times she was alert, but apprehensive, and readily admitted that the risks of shark attack in western Kansas were indeed remote!

JOHN A. ROBINSON, M.B.
ARNOLD BARNETT, M.B., M.R.C.P.
Wichita, KS   Wesley Medical Center

JAWS MODEL FOR "SMOKE"

To the Editor:

After seeing the movie *Jaws* thousands of people

stopped going to the beaches. According to the recent "Sharks and Man" convention held at Orlando, Florida, the recorded cases of shark attack average only 28 per year, world wide, since 1940. According to cancer statistics, approximately 68,000 Americans die with lung cancer every year. . . . I wonder if anyone could make a similar movie for the cigarette—he might win a prize!

AYDIN DINDOGRU, M.D.
Rochester, NY   Genesee Hospital

PONDEROUS-PURSE DISEASE

To the Editor:

. . . Ponderous-purse disease is manifest by pain, tenderness and spasm in upper-shoulder and lateral-neck muscles . . . and is sometimes accompanied by radicular pains.

. . . Constant contraction of shoulder-elevator and neck-stabilizer muscles attempting to carry the load on the side of the shouldered purse results in pain, tenderness and focal spasms of those muscles. The muscle contractions can cause abnormal neck posture and provocation of cervical-nerve radiculopathy. An informal assay of a series of feminine purse weights and contents revealed weights up to 5 kg and internal milieus that can, modestly and summarily for the uninitiated, be pursimoniously likened to the contents of a goat's stomach. The profligate-credit-card factor and coins-for-coin-eating-machines factor are links with back-pocket sciatica, but the instruments, bottles, boxes, tubes, jars, packets and spray cans of material necessary for natural beauty are unique to ponderous purses.

Prevention of ponderous-purse disease is so logical that to point it out may be considered purscilious. The physician's advice has almost no patient pursuance. An unfavored but sometimes patient-tried remedy is contralateral shifting of the shoulder purse, usually followed by contra-lateralling of the pain and needless pursponement of the cure. Switching to a hand-held purse is subjectively objectionable and objectively often complicated by purse partings, with resultant hot pursuits, purspirations and panic from loss of the beauty aids (and credit cards). Another approach, reduction of shoulder-purse contents, is apparently more of a pain in the neck than the pain in the neck. . . .

W. KING ENGEL, M.D.

Rockville, MD

THE SUNGLASS SYNDROME

To the Editor:

Last summer, I became aware of a peculiar constellation of symptoms that occurred in three women, each of whom described annoying sensations involving the suborbital area, the nose, and the upper incisors. I believe that this syndrome is not uncommon.

The three women ranged in age from 21 to 36 years, and all three described an almost identical progression of symptoms, which began in the area beneath the eyes and over the cheeks, and consisted of numbness, paresthesia, and dysesthesia. These symptoms gradually progressed to involve the nose, where the sensation was one of numbness and a peculiar dysesthesia in which air moving in and out of the nasal passages produced an uncomfortable sensation. At this stage, all three subjects believed they were coming down with a head cold. After the nasal symptoms had persisted for three or four weeks and no obvious cold had developed, the three subjects all began to notice a numbness of the upper incisors such that brush and water-picking the teeth failed to produce the expected sensation. Furthermore, when the lower incisors were brought into opposition with the upper incisors the sensation of pressure could be felt only in the lower incisors. At this point, one of the subjects consulted a dentist, because she thought that her symptoms might be related to dental disease.

It would seem that the symptoms in such patients represent a compression neuropathy. . . . The fact that the symptoms seemed to be produced by sunglasses rather than regular glasses suggests that sunglasses, which tend to be larger, are more likely to exert pressure on the area of exit of the nerve.

I have discussed these cases with several physicians, and although some of them could recollect having seen patients with similar symptoms, none had ever been able to make a diagnosis or prescribe any specific therapy. Several dentists were consulted: one was familiar with the syndrome and knew that it could be relieved by discontinuing the use of sunglasses. The fact that three patients with this syndrome were seen in a short period and that one dentist was familiar with the syndrome and knew the cause suggests that there may be a considerable number of people with the "sunglass syndrome."

GRANT R. GWINUP, B.S.
University of Arizona
Tucson, AZ   College of Medicine

IS THE UNSUIT UNSUITABLE?

To the Editor:

A new type of bathing suit has recently been released

for sale this summer. Known as the Unsuit, it is made of 100 per cent cotton with a special weave that permits the ultraviolet "tanning" rays of the sun to penetrate. This allows the wearer (as the advertising contends) to "tan where the sun doesn't shine." The manufacturer claims that the suit has a protection factor equivalent to a sunblock 6 (meaning that six times the ultraviolet radiation causing a sunburn by direct exposure of unprotected skin is required to cause a sunburn through the material).

In an attempt to measure the true protective value of the suit, several measurements of the ultraviolet B-band energy from direct sunlight were obtained . . . and compared with similar measurements of sunlight energy through the suit material. . . . Also, minimum erythema doses were computed for normally covered areas (skin of the buttocks) of two volunteers with and without the Unsuit. . . . A considerable amount of solar (and therefore carcinogenic) rays pass through the suit and strike areas of the body that are normally covered.

In the light of the above, the use of the word "protection" may be misleading. Exposure to sun is the primary risk factor for the development of skin cancer. The risk of malignant melanoma appears to be related to the number of sunburns that a person receives, especially during the teens and 20s. In fact, this risk is also increased in persons who are indoor workers with outdoor recreational habits, who tend to become sunburned in normally covered areas. The anatomical distribution of melanomas (an increase on the trunks of men and the legs of women) over normally covered areas that are at highest risk of sunburn also supports this finding. Finally, Holman (unpublished data) has shown that the risk of melanoma is related to the type of bathing suit worn by women from the age of 15 to 24. Women wearing bikinis or bathing nude had 52 times the chance of acquiring melanoma as those wearing a traditional one-piece suit, and those wearing a two-piece suit had 4 times the risk. All these findings suggest that exposing normally covered areas of the body to ultraviolet light may increase the risk of cancers of the skin, including malignant melanoma.

We therefore conclude that persons (especially those at higher risk of skin cancer) should be cautioned about the possible long-term risks associated with wearing the Unsuit.

DARRELL S. RIGEL, M.D., ALFRED W. KOPF, M.D.
DAWN I. GREENWALD, M.D., LAURIE J. LEVINE, M.D.
and ROBERT J. FRIEDMAN, M.D.
New York, NY   New York University Medical Center

INVERSION PETECHIAE

To the Editor:

I would like to report a possible complication observed in two patients who participated in inversion therapy. In this recently introduced fitness strategy, inversion boots hook the subject's ankles to a bar, allowing him to hang upside down. My observation occurred in a 34-year-old woman and a 44-year-old man with otherwise uncomplicated medical histories. Their only medication was aspirin used in the treatment of various athletic injuries. . . . The man was inverted for less than one minute while testing the unit at his local retailer. The next morning he noted periorbital petechiae.* The woman engaged in inversion for one to two minutes per day for one week, at which point she

---

*NOTE: A small round dark spot caused by bleeding into the skin or beneath the mucous membranes around the eyes.

noted periorbital petechiae. There were no other pertinent abnormalities, though formal coagulation studies were not done.

. . . Local retailers state that patients who have high blood pressure or who have had spinal fusions of uncertain stability should refrain from inversion therapy. A computer search of *Index Medicus* revealed no references concerning this subject. It seems obvious that inversion would elevate pulmonary-artery wedge pressure and also aggravate reflux esophagitis.

The observation I am reporting in these two persons may represent an additional precaution. The risk to the intracranial circulation in elderly or high-risk subjects with or without aspirin or other platelet inhibitors remains to be studied.

DAVID W. PLOCHER, M.D.
St. Paul, MN   United Hospitals of St. Paul

HIGGLEDY-PIGGLEDIES

To the Editor:

The sampling of doggerel below, most of it written late at night on the ward, or during dull conferences, may be of interest to someone on the periphery of the medical audience. . . . I might say, for the uninitiated, that the "Higgledy-Piggledy" form is a recent innovation, popularized in *Time* magazine, with the following rules (ruse?):

"1. The basic meter must be double dactyls ($/\ \smile\ \smile\ /\ \smile\ \smile$)
2. line 2 must be a proper name, in double dactyls
3. line 6 must be a single word
4. lines 7 & 8 must be a pun, joke, insight, paradox etc. etc."

Fiscal Exam

Higgledy Piggledy
Mass. General Hospital,
Helping the hapless when
Past prophylaxis,
Acme of Medicine,
panprofessorial:
Ask yourself sometimes just
Who pays the taxes.

MICHAEL M. STEWART, M.D.
Newtonville, MA

BODY SLAM IS NO SHAM

To the Editor:

Professional wrestling in America is undergoing an inexplicable, explosive growth in popularity. Enormous audiences now follow avidly a sport heretofore scourged by its critics as a sham. A recent case compels us to warn that amateur emulation of a commonly televised professional wrestling throw can have a potentially catastrophic outcome.

A 58-year-old man presented with abdominal pain of four days' duration and a vague history of a recent fall. He had no prior health problems and no gastrointestinal symptoms. Vital signs were normal. . . . Plain X-ray and computed tomographic studies suggested the presence of a large gallstone. At urgent laparotomy a ruptured gallbladder and one stone were removed. The patient recovered uneventfully. Pathological examination of the gallbladder confirmed traumatic rupture. We learned later that his son had "body slammed" him onto the lawn "doing some wrestling moves" four days before admission.

Contrary to cynical beliefs of a skeptical public, the punches and throws in a professional wrestler's armamentarium are not fakes but complex athletic/theatrical maneuvers requiring exceptional strength and coordination. One of us (J.T.L.) confirmed at ringside that opponents weighing 300 to 350 lb (135 to 169 kg) routinely survive body slams from heights of 8 ft (2.4 m). They "take the falls correctly," probably dissipating much of the force of impact into the extremities. However, many championship wrestlers are also in extraordinary physical condition and perform in a ring with a flexible floor that has a trampoline-like compliance. Our patient fortunately survived a ruptured viscus after one body slam; we calculate that his body had an initial potential energy of 1100 ft-lb and a peak velocity of almost 23 miles (37 km) per hour when it reached the unyielding turf. Deceleration/compression of the gallbladder distended by bile and a stone presumably caused longitudinal rupture of the free wall.

The authenticity of professional wrestling as a true sport will always be debated. However, the laws of physics are immutable. Spectacular television wrestling throws can generate a substantial, dangerous, and potentially lethal force. Amateurs should leave these throws to the pros.

PETER WILTON, M.B., C.CH.
JOSE FULCO, M.D.
JOHN O'LEARY, M.D.
JAMES T. LEE, M.D., PH.D
Veterans Administration
Blue Surgery Service
Minneapolis, MN

8

FLATULENCE
Intestinal Fartitude

Body language is usually silent, nonverbal communication —nodding in agreement, winking to flirt, making a fist to signal anger. But at odd times, our bodies speak up with a language of their own, a voice that can be heard, and we are out of control in a potentially distressing situation. Of course, not all unsummoned sounds are troublesome: a hiccup, cough, or sneeze, while irksome, rarely rates a blush.

Other body sounds, nonetheless, are embarrassing. Like willful children mortifying their parents, they make us squirm. We twitter and ignore stomach rumbles. But a burp butts in and demands to be noticed. And, flatulence, well, we turn up our noses at that, too. Any encounter with the volatile subject subject risks embarrassment, except in the pages of the Journal. *Physician-readers manifest an unexpected interest in the phenomenon, inflating its importance and mounting an offense in defense of their favorite four-letter word: fart. In correspondence on the subject, wit and wisdom soar to new heights in a lighter-than-air treatment.*

GOOD FOOD AND GASEOUS REPELLANTS

To the Editor:

Congratulations to M. D. Levitt ... for his study on intestinal gases. He at least heads toward establishing a norm. Observations made within a population of one family, including three physicians, spread over two generations, and a geographic extent from Boston to Portland, Oregon, has convinced me that this phenomenon is worthy of study. Dr. Levitt mentions CH_4, but not H_2S, which is a far more important expellant.

It is not at all clear why members of the brassica group of vegetables, the finest cheeses (such as Camembert, Bri[e] and even Roquefort), and the simple process of frying rather than broiling meats, when superimposed on the tensions of a strenuous medical practice, should convert a simple mix of N_2, CO_2, and CH_4 into a repellent that should have military use. What is uncertain to me is whether further research in this socially important field should be funded through NIMH or the AGA. Of all the wise men I know, only the august Editor can make this critical distinction.

PHILIP SELLING, M.C.

Portland, OR

To the Editor:

It is a shame that so many people suffer from excessive flatulence. Aside from social problems, which are bound to develop, great excesses of flatus can be uncomfortable. In a recent article by Levitt et al. we read of a serious approach to an age-old problem. We have all at one time or another had an intolerance for one kind of food or another, such as baked beans, beer or cabbage. It is rare, however, to present a patient who maintains a history of intolerance to so many foods. We may also consider that such a problem is also expensive. Levitt's patient had been seen by seven practitioners and was treated with at least five prescriptions—all to no avail. Furthermore, the patient described is still having problems. . . .

RICHARD C. BERGLUND
Chicago, IL   Rush Medical College

METHANOSIS

To the Editor:

Dr. W. C. Duane freely admits in the paper he co-authored with Dr. M. D. Levitt, "Floating Stools—Flatus versus Fat". . . that his consistently floating stools were fortuitously noted to be associated with "a CH_4 excretion rate of near record proportion." This forthright admission of a high methane rating from one of our professional colleagues inspired the following trio of limericks:

> Our thanks to frank Doctor Duane
> Who takes the time to explain
> Just how he had noted
> That his stools often floated
> Before they were flushed down the drain.

> He must have thought first, "Mama mia!
> Do I suffer from steatorrhea?
> But it cannot be that—
> There is no trace of fat."
> Which led to another idea.

> Well aware of the gas he unloosed
> The doctor quite shrewdly deduced,

(Almost clairvoyant)
His feces were buoyant
Because of the methane produced.

MILTON J. CHATTON, M.D.

San Jose, CA

NOTE:

On stools it seems all science terse
Must air itself in winks and verse.

—Ed.

FLOATERS AND SINKERS

To the Editor:

. . .

While safe's the stool that comes a sinker,
The floater's apt to be a stinker.

So it's not fat but, rather, flatus
Imparts the elevated status.

JOSEPH D. TELLER

Freehold, NJ

To the Editor:

Levitt et al. refer to hopeful recognition by the *Guiness Book of World Records* for their patient when he had "70 passages in one four-hour period" and a total of 141 in one day. Although this may be a modern record, one man, if he were alive, would certainly deflate their inflated opinion of their bombastic patient. I refer to Joseph Pujol, born in Marseilles in 1857, who became known as "Le Petomane" while in Paris performing on the Moulin Rouge stage. He became affluent for his ability not only to pass flatus but also to do imitations, most notably a 10-second aria mimicking the tearing of calico. He also did impersonations of sorts. At the peak of his career he earned over twice as much at the box office as Sarah Bernhardt. Mr. Pujol could also extinguish a candle at one foot (an unusual variation of the match test?). I think ·Dr. Levitt's patient would have been in awe of the amazing Pujol if he could have attended one of his performances. If I had been in attendance I would rather have seen Pujol imitate Marcel Marceau.

STEPHEN A. NOLLER, M.D.
Augusta, GA   ·   Medical College of Georgia

To the Editor:

...I was disappointed that certain important factors were not considered by the flatologists.... There was no mention of the duration of each passage of gas. It is a fact that the "slider" (the crowded-elevator type) lasts longer than the same one would if it were not being performed under such tight controls.

...In addition to duration, the investigators should have catalogued types. Boomer (personal communication) has reported that the open sphincter, or the "pooh" type, is of a higher temperature and is more aromatic than the "slider" or than the loud, long, staccato type pleasantly and pleasingly passed in the privacy of one's boudoir (cf. French "flatochambre"). It should be mentioned that the tighter the sphincter, the higher the pitch and the less the resonance.

Furthermore, the patient's occupation was not stated. I should be interested in the air-quality control measures taken to protect his fellow workers, particularly those in the immediate vicinity. Also, 70 passages per four hours amounts to one every 3.429 minutes—a potentially dangerous situation if one uses a welding torch or is near an open flame. If the patient worked for me, I would demand an indwelling rectal tube connected to the plant exhaust system with gas-removal equipment to stop this man's almost continuous polluting of the atmosphere.

Finally, it appears that if the *New England Journal of Medicine* continues its great interest in this fascinating new facet of medical investigative work, the headquarters should be moved from "Beantown" to "Dairyland," U.S.A.

ROBERT M. MISKIMON, M.D.
Richmond, VA   Fidelity Bankers Life Insurance Company

BLOWN OUT OF PROPORTION

To the Editor:

The impact of the studies on a flatulent patient reported by Levitt et al. . . . may be felt for years to come. I offer the following musings on what might occur as thousands of people attempt to better their patients' records, and thus become enshrined in the Guinness book.

> With records set for eating pies,
>   and swallowing fish,
>   and blinking eyes,
> The Guiness book has set its sights
>   on one of man's
>   most private rights.
>
> And as the flatus record's passed,
>   who knows how many
>   will be gassed?
> Who knows what changes will appear
>   in content of
>   the atmosphere?

As standards fall and odors rise
    till everyone
    has tearing eyes,
We may all have to make our homes
    in specially filtered
    gas-proof domes.

And soon flatulence's greatest names
    may gather at
    the Olympic games
Trying with each mighty crack
    to blow opponents
    off the track.

MICHAEL S. PALMER, M.D.
Falmouth, MA   Falmouth Medical Associates

PLAIN WORDS FOR "PASSED FLATUS"

To the Editor:

   . . . There seems to be a curious omission on this subject both in the literature and in the English language. I do not recall any relevant treatise in the psychiatric literature and I do not know of any commonly used single word in the English language that means "pass flatus"—with the exception of a four-letter word.

   This four-letter word is "fart," which is both a verb and a noun. Such awkward phrases as "passed flatus" or "excreted gas" are always used instead of "farted." And a "fart"—as a noun—can be visualized on x-ray.

   It is also curiously interesting that concerning the other (upper) end of the gastrointestinal tract, the language does not have usable single words: to belch and a belch, as well as to erupt and an eructation. The word "fart" appreciably arouses more feelings of disgust than the words "expelled flatus" or "belch."

The matter gets curiouser and curiouser in our wonderland and I am awaiting etymologic studies on these words and psychological studies on a suitable patient.

ROBERT J.L. WAUGH, M.D.
Ward's Island, NY   Dunlap–Manhattan Psychiatric Center

To the Editor:

> Psychiatrist Waugh
> Makes the complaint
> That medical writers
> Are bound by restraint.
>
> To use technical terms
> For everyday facts,
> And circumlocutions
> For natural acts.
>
> Perhaps we should drop
> Superfluous fetters,
> And turn to plain words
> With only four letters.
>
> As a matter of fact,
> The state of the art
> Deprives us of words
> Even better than fart.
>
> Yes, Doctor Waugh,
> Where is there logic,
> In medical matters,
> Etymologic?

MILTON J. CHATTON, M.D.
San Jose, CA   Department of Rehabilitation

To the Editor:

The observation by Dr. Waugh that the English language contains several synonyms for eructation but none (except the well-known vulgarism) for flatus demonstrates the universality of anal-related repression and distortion mechanisms. The very fact that the vulgar term for flatus generates much stronger feelings than the slang word "burp" illustrates the psychological implications of these processes. What I am really referring to is a cause-and-effect relation between these mechanisms and the presence or absence of both polite conversational words and vulgarisms in the English vocabulary. There are many and varied acceptable outlets for oral expression (eating, drinking, kissing, talking, facial expression, etc.), but anal expression is something else altogether.

We have all observed persons who actually seem to thrive on their capacity to make numerous and imaginative anal-erotic references to virtually every life situation they encounter. Where would these people be without their anal vulgarisms?

Many of us, however, find more refined devices than frequent use of vulgarity. In *The Psychopathology of Everyday Life*, Freud explored the psychodynamics of wit and explained how the best jokes deal with repressed material through distortion and double entendre. I chuckled (as I'm sure most other readers of the original article on flatus did) over the "whiff-of-success" quip that concluded the author's remarks. Our concern about the neurotic sequelae of repression sometimes precludes our recognition of its more positive consequences. Wit and humor certainly belong in the latter category.

RICHARD WILEY FARDY

Billerica, MA

To the Editor:

A discussion of the relative merits of the words that we employ to describe our gaseous intestinal discharges is a light subject to be sure. Any conversation dealing with such subjects invariably degenerates to joke making and is promptly forgotten. However, in the light of Dr. Waugh's comments, I am compelled to respond.

The act of passing flatus is most distinctly described by the word crepitation. This word, I am sure, Dr. Waugh will find far more esthetically pleasing than the four-letter word to which he refers in his letter. The only drawback to this choice is its obvious similarity to another well-chosen four-letter word, which, if he were alive today, might lead to certain psychosocial difficulties for Thomas Crapper, without whose guidance and inventiveness we might all still be soiling our shoes.

If that won't suffice, I might suggest "exmeterorate" (meterorism being the state of having gas in one's intestine), which has no foul or fecal connotations. In any event, no matter which word you prefer, this entire dialogue, seen by thousands of physicians and students in a highly respected publication, will remain on these pages nothing more than a fleeting farce.

MARK SILEN
Boston, MA   Harvard Medical School

NOTE: *Other synonyms suggested are "BM burp," "exogust," "flatulate," and "boomerate."* —Ed.

To the Editor:

I agree with Dr. Waugh . . . but I fail to see why he is so upset. . . . There are a number of verb phrases in the English language, connoting actions considered both unpleasant and pleasant, for which a similar situation exists, many of which are used in everyday medical care.

The best example I can think of offhand is "engage in sexual intercourse." A number of words of three, four, and five letters are well known to the lay (sic) and medical public and need not be printed here. In addition, there are "have sex," "make love," "have intercourse" and "do it." The only single usable word is "fornicate," which both is distressingly awkward and implies activity taking place predominantly under arches. (Would D. Waugh, as a psychiatrist, ask one of his patients with sexual dysfunction, "Well, how often do you fornicate without difficulty?")

And while we're on the subject of sex, is there a single-word synonym for "attain an erection" other than "erect"? (To say, "I erect readily," when you mean, "I don't have trouble getting hard," is about as graceful as saying, "I eruct readily," when you mean, "I belch a lot.")

To satisfy Dr. Waugh's monoverbomania regarding "pass flatus," I would offer "deflate" as both pleasing to the ear and etymologically satisfying, but I think he makes excessive demands on our vocabulary. I suspect that the "suitable patient for psychologic study" whom he seeks will in the end probably turn out to be an old fart.

GILBERT BRODSKY
Boston, MA   Harvard Medical School

To the Editor:

For many years, I have entertained friends by giving them the derivation of four-letter words. Dr. Waugh's quaint comments concerning a plain word for "passed flatus" ... encourage me to share my background in the classics with a larger audience.

The word "fart" is derived from the Greek word "perdesthai." The ending "esthai" is a standard Greek ending and irrelevant. The foot "perd" is critical. As all students of language know, "p" is often changed to "ph," which then becomes "f" (the Greeks had no letter "h"). The change of the vowel "e" to "a" and of the soft "d" to the staccato "t" is hardly surprising. Thus, "perd" equals "fart."

It is surprising that this information is not widely known, since it is available in any unabridged English dictionary. Some may be interested to know that the Greek word perdesthai is ferociously irregular in its conjunction, with an aorist that hardly resembles the root word. I agree with Dr. Waugh that it is curious that most dictionaries refer to the word as "slang," and the *Oxford English Dictionary* states "not now in decent use," before giving many examples from the classical English literature.

ERIC REISS, M.D.
University of Miami
Miami, FL   School of Medicine

FINAL OUTBURST

To the Editor:

The volume of correspondence inspired by the article on a flatulent patient . . . has become quite inflated. I do wish, however, to add this further comment . . . on the difficulty of finding an acceptable word for "passed flatus."

The simplest English words describing emunctory functions—whether the excretion of gas, fluid or solid—are all of four letters and one syllable, and are quite ancient. They date from a time when excretion could be mentioned without disguise. Thus, the word "fart" was used by Chaucer in the "Miller's Tale" (in 1386?) and no other word or euphemism would have proved as effective in conveying the impact of one episode of that story. Now, although "fart" and similar words are listed in the *Oxford English Dictionary*, the *Dictionary* very carefully states that "fart" is "not in decent use." Perhaps what is needed is a better definition of "decent."

HENRY J. TUMEN, M.D.

Philadelphia, PA

To the Editor:

. . . As a student of Washington etymology I suggest "Flatus Advance by Rectal Transport." For which that perfectly acceptable form, the acronym, would be, naturally, "FART."

VICTOR COHN

Washington, DC   *Washington Post*

SPEAKING THE UNSPEAKABLE

To the Editor:

This letter is to make it official. The word fart was used factually, without embarrassment at 1310 hours on Wednesday, May 17, in Lecture Room B, University Hospital, during a lecture to the second-year medical class on "Gaseousness." I was encouraged to use the term by the recent correspondence on the matter in the *Journal*. I am essentially a religious God-fearing man, an avoider of obscenities and a lover of the English language. On due reflection I was persuaded of the intrinsic value of this word and of its non-offensiveness. The students have been encouraged to use it freely where clinically appropriate. Not unnaturally, there were a few titters; indeed, it would be true to say there were even a few guffaws at first. But once the word had been used a few times it came to sound natural and as unremarkable as any other suitable clinical term.

I hope that all other clinicians, men of honor and upright standing, will follow this lead. A spark has been struck; a torch has been lit. Let it shine forth and illumine the dark recesses of what has hitherto been that unspeakable thing.

I am, acknowledging the encouragement of the *Journal*, with fart healt thanks.

W. C. WATSON, M.D.
London, Canada   Victoria Hospital

To the Editor:

Dr. Watson documents his making "official" the unabashed use of the word fart in formal medical discourse and notes that, in consequence, "a torch has been lit." One may assume the fuel to be largely methane.

Among untold other benefits perhaps this pioneering effort will free us to name several formerly indefinite syndromes of gastrointestinal uneasiness—e.g., the patient with "gas pains" and bloating who has had difficulty in expelling the cause of his malaise. For this one, I propose "congestive fart failure."

DAVID H. SPODICK, M.D., D.SC.
Worcester, MA   St. Vincent Hospital

9

FLUKES
Green Is the Color
of My True Love's Hair

Flukes are practical jokes life plays with assumptions. A rational universe that behaves predictably, however, is the keystone of most science—pi always equals 3.14159 . . . , water everywhere is H_2O, and astronomers viewing stars over Alabama see the same constellations as astronomers in Zimbabwe. Medical science, on the contrary, encounters many flukes.

Human hair is usually blond, brown, black, red, white, gray, or some shade in between. Green hair is a fluke.

Food may be burning hot or spicy hot, but if taking a bite kindles sparks, that's a fluke.

And when a patient notifies his physician that a side effect of a prescribed medication affects his watch, it's time to talk about the tic.

Correspondence in the Journal *examines medical flukes, often operates as a dispensary for explanations, and sometimes prescribes a remedy.*

THE MAN WITH GREEN HAIR

To the Editor:

We hope someone can help us solve the following problem.

A 51-year-old mentally retarded man with phenylketonuria has had patches of green, only in his scalp hair, for several years. The color intensity varies from bright, light green to being barely visible. It is visible within 1 cm. of the scalp and extends out to 2 to 3 cm. with the remainder of the shaft blond or gray. Usually, he has had one or two patches 1 to 3 cm. in diameter, which vary in location, but are most common over the parietal area. He has been on no medication. His hair has been washed daily with soap and at least once a week with a non-tar shampoo. On some occasions shampoo has appeared to remove some of the green color. He is under close observation at the Walter E. Fernald State School and has never been observed to rub his head on objects or rub material into his hair. . . .

LEWIS B. HOLMES, M.D.
Boston, MA   Massachusetts General Hospital

LOWELL A. GOLDSMITH, M.D.
Durham, NC   Duke University Medical Center

To the Editor:

Drs. Holmes and Goldsmith . . . have raised an interesting question about the man with green hair. Although I can locate no recent work on the subject, a current textbook on dermatology does make mention of Beigel's work in Germany of 1867, when he found that copper workers often had green hair.

In a short review of the subject in 1882, T. Colcott Fox

noted: "On the forehead the copper particles in the man's environment would be able to settle; not so in the hair from under the jaw. In the hairs from scalp the points showed a gray-green color quite intense for 3 cm., but, further from the tips the color gradually disappeared, til at the 10 cm. there was only a gray-white color." Copper could be shown from the hairs by the ammonia blue color test.

Two years later, George Jackson wrote that the green color becomes deeper each year in copper workers. "The color can be entirely washed out," the New York dermatologist stated, "and the microscope shows that it is from without and not from within the hair."

Gould and Pyle, in the *Anomalies and Curiosities of Medicine*, reported green hair in both copper and brass workers, but could offer no explanation for this change in color.

It seems that the patient of Dr. Holmes and Goldsmith had come in contact with copper compound. Could this contact have been from an instrument used as a comb? Are there copper-producing factories in the area that emit fumes?

LAWRENCE CHARLES PARISH, M.D.
University of Pennsylvania
Philadelphia, PA   School of Medicine

To the Editor:

Light may be thrown on the problem of "The Man with Green Hair" . . . by consideration of a minor epidemic of green hair in Framingham, Massachusetts, a few years ago. The problem was particularly acute in the Framingham State College, where there is a large group of girls with blond hair, who, unlike the subject in the above men-

tioned letter, were neither phenylketonuric nor retarded.
Blondes were mainly affected. The green-hair problem
started after the introduction of fluoride into the town water
supply. The type of fluoride used changed the pH of the
water from between 7.5 and 8.5 to about 5.8. The acidified
water drew copper from household piping, the copper then
being deposited on the hair during shampooing. One of us
(JG) saw a blond adolescent girl, living [in] a neighboring
town, who had a similar problem. This town had its own
wells, and the water supply was fluoridated. The green hair
resulted in several reports in *The South Middlesex Daily
News* before the problem was recognized and solved by
changing the pH of the water back to its usual range by the
addition of sodium hydroxide. . . .

This letter should neither mark us as opponents of fluoridation, of which we are strong supporters, nor furnish
comfort and support to the opponents of fluoridation.

ROBERT COOPER, B.A.
JOSEPH GOODMAN, M.D.
Framingham, MA

GREEN ASPIRIN

To the Editor:

Years ago I was physician to a select girls school and the
following observations were made. On a spring day I was
going over with the school nurse supply orders for the ensuing year when she asked me, "Can't I have anything
better for dysmenorrhea than aspirin?" My answer was,
"No. Our girls all have their own physicians, and anything
other than immediate treatment should be handled by them
and not the school." But she was persistent: "Even the

teachers come to me for something to give them relief." By that time I was bored and exasperated and said, "Oh, h——, get some green aspirin," and promptly forgot it.

The next fall, when I was doing routine physical examinations, a girl came in doubled up, saying, "Mrs. A., I have such terrible cramps." To my amazement and horror, Mrs. A. took out a 1000 tablet bottle of green aspirin, with a label easily read across the room which said: "Dr. G's Special RX for Cramps." She gave the child one tablet to be taken with a full glass of water, and told her to return in two hours—which she did, reporting that she felt fine, having been in class during the interval. While Mrs. A was with us the treatment was continued; students and teachers proclaimed it "the best." The payoff came one evening when I was called by a doctor friend, who said, "You don't have to answer, but tonight my daughter has such bad cramps that nothing I've given her—even codeine—has helped: and she insists that the only thing that helps is what she gets at school." I told him and added, "Please don't tell her yet, because we are still using it." His response: "Green aspirin—good God, I'll get some pronto, and it gives me insight into my daughter's problems."

Why was the green aspirin effective? That particular nurse had the ability to convince her victims that the remedy was effective, combined with the physiologic fact that menstrual cramps are self-healing within two or three hours with or without treatment, especially if the patient goes about her usual routine.

After the green aspirin was discontinued with the advent of a nurse who was a down-to-earth New Englander, a graduate of the M.G.H. and the Children's, I told the assembled students and teachers about it. The horror, consternation, disbelief, and glee on the faces of my audience were delightful to see.

(My husband, a retired surgeon, has reminded me to

note that the male of the species has also been known to respond to the green-aspirin effect.)

LEONA V. GLOVER, M.D.

Cleveland, OH

WINTERGREEN MINTS ESCHEWED

To the Editor:

Many discoveries have been made in bed. Few of these discoveries are new, and fewer bear reporting.

We admit that this is only a report of a study in progress, and this could easily be the end of our progress. Finding the time for a research project in a rural community is sometimes something of a task. The purpose of the report is to create a wide audience of medical interest in the hope that the problem will be carried to completion. . . .

One night as one of us and his wife were just drifting off to sleep, their daughter bounced into the darkened bedroom and asked if they would like to see what she learned at the University of Nebraska. He always wanted to know what his tuition was going for, so naturally he was eager to see what she learned, expecting something very cultural that she had possibly missed in Illinois. She proceeded to demonstrate how you can bite hard on a dry wintergreen mint and produce a spark. She had not learned this in a class; she had learned it in her dormitory. We have repeated this experiment successfully many numbers of times. We have learned that wintergreen "Certs" work nicely, but our research has been limited mostly to the brand "Life Savers."
. . . We suggest that you stand before a mirror in total darkness and chomp down on one. Perhaps many youngsters are aware of this phenomenon, but we are sure the medical profession is generally unaware of it. At first, this

would seem to have no clinical importance, but obviously a spark in the operating room in an area of cyclopropane or ether would have dire consequences.

We tried to photograph the spark with a very sensitive film . . . but could not produce enough light to register. . . . Perhaps the static electricity so produced is not great enough to cause an explosion. We lack the courage to attempt this in an atmosphere of pure oxygen or with cyclopropane. We would be interested in the results of anyone . . . brave enough to try. . . .

It appears to us that wintergreen-mint chewing may be a hazard and, until proved otherwise, should be discouraged in explosive atmospheres. . . . We would never want to think that a spacecraft exploded because an astronaut inadvertently chewed a wintergreen mint.

HOWARD EDWARDS, JR., M.D.
DONALD W. EDWARDS, M.D.
Dixon, IL   Edwards Clinic

To the Editor:

The warning . . . concerning the possible hazard of chewing wintergreen mints in the presence of explosive gases is commendable but may be unnecessarily alarming to the profession.

A transient luminescence, presumably triboluminescence of relatively low energy, is produced by the breaking or grating of sugar crystals, and has been known for some years. More recently Harvey pointed out the enhanced triboluminescence of wintergreen flavored "Neccos" in contrast to those flavored with lemon, lime, clove, sassafras, cinnamon, chocolate or licorice or with no flavoring at all. Such luminescence is probably insuffi-

cient to strike a spark other than in the curiosity of the
observer. . . .

ROBERT WADE SPEIR, M.D.
Yale University School of Medicine
New Haven, CT   Yale Arbovirus Research Unit

To the Editor:
Many thanks to the Doctors Edwards. . . . Their comments provoked a good deal of nocturnal hilarity and probably a large boost in the sale of wintergreen mints locally
as the entertainment spread into the local prep school.

I am now in a position to add that spearmints produce a
much weaker but discernible light and that both work
equally well when the mint is tapped by a hammer. The
hammer technic spares the experimenter the nausea resulting from disposal of the chewed mint. . . .

JEROME T. NOLAN, M.D.
Exeter, NH   Exeter Clinic

EUCHARISTIC PROBLEMS FOR CELIAC PATIENTS

To the Editor:
. . . The intestinal mucosa of patients with celiac disease
is very sensitive even to small amounts of gluten in the
diet. Because of the presence of wheat in the Host, this
may be a real problem for Catholic adolescents with celiac
disease who attend holy communion regularly. We are following an eight-year-old boy with growth retardation and a
flat intestinal mucosa, who after six months of a gluten-
free regimen celebrated his first holy communion; thereafter, he took holy communion once a week and showed
unsatisfactory growth. A second intestinal biopsy, carried

out six months after the first communion, showed a partial villous atrophy, notwithstanding the absence of gluten in the diet on detailed dietary inquiry. A third intestinal biopsy was performed after three months, when the child was no longer taking communion, the intestinal mucosa was normal, and the child began growing. We suggest that the presence of gluten in the Host may be overlooked by physicians, who may infer another dietary source of gluten or the need for another diagnosis. The problem is amplified for patients with celiac disease who attend Catholic schools, because they take communion frequently. According to the New Testament a wheat-free Host is unacceptable, but it might be theologically acceptable for patients with celiac disease to take holy communion in the form of Christ's blood (consecrated wine) instead of his body.

MARIA SERENELLA SCOTTA, CONTANTINO DE GIACOMO,
GUISEPPE MAGGIORE, SALVATORE SIENA,
AND ALBERTO G. UGAZIO
Pavia, Italy   University of Pavia

HASHISHECTOMY

To the Editor:

On May 9, 1970, during the Demonstration and march on Washington by antiwar protestors, a young lady of 18 removed her clothing and waded in the reflecting pool in front of the Lincoln Memorial with a host of her friends and associates. She was in possession of 0.5 g of hashish entrusted to her care by her friends. Rather than risk the loss of the hashish if her clothes were stolen, she placed it in her left ear. She was apparently splashed, the hashish became wet, and she was unable to extract it. A friend came to her aid, but only succeeded in impacting the foreign body well into the external auditory canal. The patient was taken to the Emergency Room of George Washington University Hospital, where it was noted that the left external auditory canal was occluded by a wad of material that would otherwise have been indistinguishable from cerumen. Her responses were noted to be slow, and she admitted to being "high" although she had not smoked either marijuana or hashish that day. The foreign body was successfully removed (hashishectomy), and returned to the patient, presumably to be smoked by her and her friends that night.

This experience suggests that tetrahydrocannabinol, the active ingredient of hashish, can be absorbed from the epithelium of the external auditory canal.

THOMAS E. PIEMME, M.D.
George Washington University
Washington, DC   School of Medicine

SMOOTH TOBACCO AND WRINKLED SKIN

To the Editor:

This note is to call attention to an observation that would seem to be of some importance to many of the *Journal* readers.

There must be a close relation between the presence of wrinkling of the facial skin and habitual cigarette smoking. The relation first became apparent to be several years ago and has become increasingly impressive to me since that time.

Others, to whom I have mentioned the relation, skeptical at first, have returned, exclaiming with great enthusiasm, "It's true, it's true." I have found no mention of the relation in textbooks and no reference confirming the observation.

Needless to say, it has been of miraculous assistance in encouraging my female patients to stop smoking. Heart-to-heart talks and threats of catastrophic disease, delivered with a grave-countenance, have been of little effect compared to the diagnosis of "impending crow's-feet."

HARRY W. DANIELL, M.D.
Redding, CA

"LIPSTICK-ON-TEETH" SIGN IN SJÖGREN'S SYNDROME

To the Editor:

Sjögren's syndrome is a chronic autoimmune disorder ... that leads to a reduction or absence of glandular secretions as well as to mucosal dryness. ...

As a physician involved in both internal medicine and hematology, I have been surprised by the frequency with which women with either primary or secondary Sjögren's syndrome either have or describe an unusual adherence of lipstick to their teeth, mainly on the upper incisors. Since most lipsticks have hydrophobic vehicles, they do not ordinarily stick to teeth; however, when the production of saliva is impaired, lipstick that is placed on the lips can easily stick to dry, unlubricated teeth. I have noticed this sign in most of my patients with Sjögren's syndrome. Other causes of the "lipstick-on-teeth" sign are drug-induced impaired production of saliva, as with ingestion of tricyclic antidepressants, or dehydration, as in hyperglycemia. When these easily identified conditions are ruled out, the "lipstick-on-teeth" sign may alert physicians to the presence of Sjögren's syndrome.

GUILLERMO J. RUIZ-ARGUELLES, M.D.
Puebla, Mexico   Hematologia y Medicina Interna

COSMETIC BENEFIT OF
ELECTROCARDIOGRAPHIC ELECTRODE

To the Editor:

Isaac Newton saw an apple fall and worked out the law of gravity; that was important. Alexander Fleming noticed that a culture did not grow as expected, and discovered the use of penicillin; that was important. A 49-year-old woman had a coronary occlusion, was monitored in our coronary-care unit and discovered something completely unrelated to a myocardial infarction that to her was extremely important, outranking penicillin and gravity. During the first three days after she was admitted, she was monitored constantly by electrocardiograph, with disposable pads placed routinely on the anterior chest wall. She did well, and on the fourth day I discontinued the monitoring. When the nurse came in that morning to clean her up, part of the clean-up job consisted in removing the disposable foam-rubber electrodes.

The patient promptly protested, exclaiming vehemently, "Where's my hickey?" A little investigation revealed that the patient wanted another disposable monitoring electrode for a very valid reason. Four years previously she had come to my office with a lump in one breast that turned out to be cancer and resulted in a prompt mastectomy. Thus far she has done well after the breast operation, except for one thing. Psychologically her recovery was excellent, and she obtained a well formed prosthesis that fitted inside her brassiere well and matched the other breast extremely well. Except that she is a bit on the obese side, and whenever she would sit down, her abdomen would push up on her brassiere and displace the prosthesis upward about 5 cm, and embarrass her inordinately. To try to hold the brassiere in place, she tried tape of all sorts, pins, stitching, or what have you. After the coronary occlusion she discovered that the electrocardiographic electrode, when placed properly on her operated side of the chest wall, held her brassiere in place, no matter what position she put herself in. She tucked the lower 0.6 cm of her brassiere under the lower part of the electrode, and everything stayed in place, come hell or high stomach.

LEONARD M. ECKMANN, M.D.
South Charleston, WV

CARSONOGENOUS MONOCULAR NYCTALOPIA

To the Editor:

A 30-year-old woman was referred to me because of left-sided night blindness. Since I had had the same disorder recently, I was interested in determining whether the circumstances were the same.

She noticed the problem after turning off the television in her bedroom. She customarily watched a popular late evening talk show while lying prone in bed, with her head turned to the left and her right eye buried in the pillow. Naturally, when it came time to turn off the set she could see well only with the dark-adapted, right eye. The problem was explained and she was relieved.

J. PARK BIEHL, M.D.
Cincinnati, OH

BLINKING VALVE

To the Editor:

We should like to describe an ocular sign of an aortic-valve prosthesis.

A patient was observed to have a rapid eye blink, at a rate of 72 per minute. The eye blinking was synchronous with the loud clicking of his aortic-valve prosthesis. Upon inquiry, he was unaware of the presence of his blinking but had complete conscious control over it. Blinking may represent a conditioned response to the continuous auditory and vibratory stimulus resulting from the prosthesis.

CHRISTOPHER P. KHOURY, B.A.
LEE C. AREA, B.S.
THOMAS DUGAN, M.D.
Durham, NC   Duke Hospital

A CLOSE ENCOUNTER OF THE BREAST KIND

To the Editor:

The cover title of the article by Higginbottom, Sweetman, and Nyhan in the August 17 issue of the *Journal* was most intriguing. I began to think either that "we are not alone" or that Isaac Asimov has been writing for the *Journal*. My encyclopedia says that "Vega" is the brightest star in the constellation "Lyra," and it is only 26 light-years from Earth. Do nursing vegans have a set of parallel breasts, or are they marsupials with vest-pocket breasts?

Vegans, if you are trying to communicate with us through the *New England Journal of Medicine*, we are friendly.

What chagrin, therefore, to turn to the article itself and discover that "vegan" means "strict vegetarian"!

NADYA K. BLEISCH, M.D.
St. Louis, MO

LONG-LASTING VISUAL AFTEREFFECT FROM VIEWING A COMPUTER VIDEO DISPLAY

To the Editor:

We recently noticed an unusual and vivid visual illusion produced by working with an IBM personal computer. This unit has a video display that presents luminous green characters on a dark background. After a session at the computer, ordinary white letters and lines on a contrasting background appear to have a pink color. A broad expanse of white, such as a sheet of paper or a white wall, does not appear to have the illusory tint, although a pink fringe may be seen at its edge. The color is most evident in figures whose elements have dimensions similar (in terms of visual angle) to those of the characters on the computer display. Several hours of work at the video screen gave rise to a very striking aftereffect, which may persist for an entire day or longer. Shorter exposures produce a less intense but still obvious effect.

The illusion is an example of the so-called McCollough effect, a phenomenon well known to psychologists. Its physiologic mechanism appears to be fundamentally different from that responsible for the more familiar afterimages produced by staring at any intensely colored object. The McCollough effect is generally believed to arise from adaptation of cortical neurons responsive to specific combinations of color and form. Afterimages, in contrast, are thought to originate in the retina. A unique feature of the McCollough effect is its long duration, which may be as great as several weeks after experimental induction. To our knowledge it is never permanent. . . .

MARK J. GREENWALD, M.D.
SUSAN L. GREENWALD, M. ARCH.
RANDOLPH BLAKE, PH.D.
Chicago, IL   Northwestern University

TELEPHONE TRANSMISSION OF HEPATITIS B?

To the Editor:

Saturating medical literature in recent years has been speculation about a remarkable variety of theoretical transmission mechanisms for the hepatitis B virus. Interestingly enough, investigators have incriminated infusion, illicit injection, inapparent inoculations, ingestion, intercourse, intimacy, insects, and, ironically, icteric illness from eye instillation of the infectious ichor. A recent report has gone so far as to imply that even nuns, although not habit-ually important in disease dissemination, may have a greater propensity to serologic evidence by hepatitis B infection than prostitutes from the same urban area.

In the presence of a telephone survey of transfusion recipients of a possibly contaminated commercial blood product, one of us (D.B.N.), after multiple telephone calls during a single day, noted the gradual onset of lethargy, malaise, headache, otalgia, low back pain, gluteal rash, profound anorexia, and a growing sensation in the upper abdomen. . . . There was no diminished taste for cigarettes or coffee. In an attempt to relieve these distressing symptoms, the interviewer medicated himself with a sizable quantity of ethanol. This therapeutic modality temporarily ameliorated the symptoms—dry mouth, nausea, and a slight darkening of the urine. A transaminase in serum drawn at the time was slightly elevated. . . .

Because of the nature of the telephone contacts, we have reason to believe that this case may represent the first report of telephone transmission of hepatitis B. The unusually short incubation period seen in this case may reflect the speed of sound, with the virus somehow traveling synergistically within this framework. . . .

A bell-shape curve of the epidemic has confirmed our hypothesis, and all reputable investigators have been tapped for further ideas. We would willingly discuss our data by telephone with any interested antigen-negative person.

CHARLES P. PATTISON, M.D.
Phoenix, AR   Center for Disease Control

DAVID B. NELSON, M.D.
CALVIN A. KLEIN, M.D.
Atlanta, GA   Center for Disease Control

To the Editor:

Drs. Pattison, Nelson and Klein ... postulate the telephonic transmission of ultra-short-incubation Type B viral hepatitis, presumably via the oral-aural route. Although their conjecture is expressed with all-inclusive alliteration and artful humor, they overlook a more likely cause of the telephone transmission of normal incubation Type B hepatitis. HB_sAg has been found in a large fraction of patients. . . . The contamination of telephone mouthpieces is almost inevitable, and telephones must be added to the list of fomites. If gonorrhea can be transmitted by toilet seats, as many victims have long claimed, the concept of the transmission of hepatitis by a telephone transmitter should be easily acceptable. Furthermore, one might postulate that telephone conversations are responsible for the transmission of more hepatitis than all cases due to blood transfusions, shared needles, oral intimacies and sexual unions. In suppressing the spread of hepatitis, one must interdict another of the primary human needs ... the need to yak. In addition, one must consider disposable telephone masks, an easy system for sterilizing telephones or, if all else fails, a self-destructing telephone.

HAROLD O. CONN, M.D.
West Haven, CT   Veterans Administration Hospital

To the Editor:

I suppose that the letter, "Telephone Transmission of Hepatitis B?" was printed as a light diversion from current worldly difficulties.

I cannot believe that the authors think that a virus can travel at the speed of light (not sound), decelerate at dozens of relays, and then, being so envigorated from contact with Ma Bell, that it rematerializes in the electromagnet of the ear piece and jumps, with the speed of sound, into the listener's ear. The trip also appeared to have enhanced the virus's infectivity so greatly that the incubation period was reduced to a few hours.

DAVID B. KESSLER, M.D.
Silver Spring, MD

To the Editor:

...It's good to know that editors of American... scientific journals allow a little impishness to appear in their publications! However, as a stockholder, I should resent the implication that spread of disease is now added to the "Bell" system's alleged crimes.

RALPH E. WHEELER, M.D.
Medford, MA   Tufts University

ALLERGY TO SEMINAL FLUID

To the Editor:

An allergic reaction against constituents of normal seminal plasma is a rare event. We have recently seen a patient who had such a reaction. She is a 25-year-old woman with familial atopic disease. Her maternal grandfather, her mother, one sister and the patient suffer from allergic asthma. Three years ago, after sexual intercourse, she noticed severe urticaria, periorbital swelling and abdominal cramps. These symptoms recurred after each intercourse and increased in intensity; at one occasion she had a circulatory collapse. When a condom was used she remained free of allergic symptoms.

Intracutaneous testing demonstrated that the responsible antigen was a constituent of seminal plasma and was not associated with spermatozoa. . . .

In order to compare our results to those previously reported an attempt was made to characterize the responsible component.

. . . Halpern's and our patient had familial atopic disease, and the third woman had ragweed hay fever of 15 years' duration. The substance responsible for the reaction is a constituent of the normal seminal fluid, probably a protein. We do not know whether, in all three cases, we are dealing with the same active compound. . . . This consideration implies the existence of a male-specific protein in genital secretions. In addition one may consider the alternative hypothesis that a factor usually present in the secretions of the genital tract in males and females is absent in the three patients. This situation, in addition to the different immune response, thought to be present in atopic disease, could lead to the development of this rare type of allergic reaction.

K. H. Schulz
C. Schirren
Hamburg, Germany   Universitas-Hautklinik

F. Kueppers
Rochester, MN   Mayo Clinic

SEXUAL INTERCOURSE AND
TRANSIENT GLOBAL AMNESIA

To the Editor:

The syndrome of transient global amnesia is manifested by an abrupt onset of profound memory loss and disorientation without change in consciousness. The episodes last for several hours, but memory gradually returns to normal. . . . I saw two patients who reported typical episodes of this amnesia after sexual intercourse with their respective spouses.

A 64-year-old woman with hypertension had noted the onset of visual blurring and an associated scotoma in the right visual field five months before admission. One month before admission, after sexual intercourse with her husband, she suddenly experienced confusion and disorientation and could not recognize her surroundings. Twelve hours later, her mental state returned to normal. She had noted a similar brief episode approximately three weeks earlier. Physical examination was unremarkable, and I found no evidence of aphasia or memory disturbance. Computerized tomography of the head and electroencephalographic findings were unremarkable. The patient has been able to return to her usual activities, including sexual relations with her husband, and is asymptomatic.

A 47-year-old man had a two-year history of moderate hypertension, yet had been in excellent health before the day of admission. Ten hours earlier, his wife found him in a state of confusion wandering around the house, just after completing sexual intercourse. On questioning him, his wife found him disoriented to location, time and date. He was unable to recall events of the previous day. The patient's blood pressure on admission was 190/120 mg Hg.

and there was a slight cardiomegaly. He was alert, attentive, oriented to place and person and had no aphasia or memory disturbance, except for the period of transient global amnesia. Computerized tomography of the head, lumbar puncture and electroenphalographic findings were unremarkable. The patient recovered within 24 hours and has resumed his usual activities, including sexual relations with his wife.

. . . Transient global amnesia has a favorable prognosis, and most patients experience only a single episode. Therefore, one need not discourage such patients from resuming their normal sexual activities.

RICHARD MAYEUX, M.D.
New York, NY   Neurological Institute

CENTENARIAN HAND SYNDROME

To the Editor:

We recently cared for a 100-year-old man with acute tenosynovitis of the right wrist and hand; his history was of interest and suggested a new syndrome to us.

This gentleman had been stable until 48 hours before his presentation. At that time, he had attended a birthday party (100th) in his honor held at the town hall. A large number of friends and relatives in attendance had shaken his hand in congratulation as he sat comfortably in his wheelchair.

The next day, he awakened with pain, swelling, and erythema of the right wrist and hand; X-ray examination did not show a fracture, and the clinical findings were consistent with tenosynovitis.

Since similar celebrations occur around the world, the

chance of similar consequences exists. We propose the centenarian hand syndrome as a name for this disorder.

ROBERT WEBB, M.D.
L. M. WILLIAMS, M.D.
Charles Town, WV

"WATCH THAT TREMOR"

To the Editor:

I was very much interested in the *Journal*'s paper on the L-dopa treatment of Parkinson's disease. I recently started using this drug at the Graduate Hospital, University of Pennsylvania, and ran into a very important side effect during the second week. One of the patients notified me that his self-winding wrist watch stopped because of the markedly diminished tremor of the left upper extremity that had been winding his watch automatically for several years. I thought readers might be interested in hearing of this unique side effect of the drug.

ARNOLD SADWIN, M.D.
Philadelphia, PA

To the Editor:

I was amused at Dr. Arnold Sadwin's letter about L-dopa interfering with the tremor efficiency of watch-winding.

Some years ago we asked the Hamilton Watch Company to make a self-winder that would work directly on the hour and minute hand so that a patient with Parkinson's disease could have his tremor measured over an hour or so. They presented our laboratory with a fine wristwatch on a good-looking wristband that measured tremor. When quiet, it was quiet too. There were no works or mainspring. It didn't tell time. We used it for a month—severe tremor over an hour indicated by eight hours and 30 minutes, and mild by 20 minutes or so. It promised to be clinically useful. One morning it was stolen. A little satisfaction was gained from the picture of the thief trying to use it as a timepiece and finally the puzzled look of the watchmaker who saw no works therein. . . .

ROBERT S. SCHWAB, M.D.
Boston, MA   Massachusetts General Hospital

MEDICINE FOR MATURE VIEWERS

To the Editor:

A recent advertisement from the entertainment section of the *Los Angeles Times* is shown. . . .

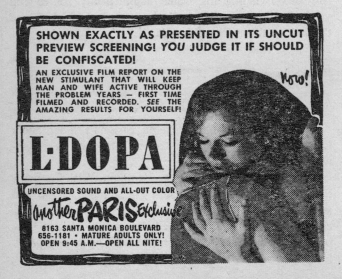

Courtesy, *Los Angeles Times*

Obviously, the film makers of today are more widely read than their predecessors. Little did James Parkinson realize in 1817 that he would be part of the sexual revolution. . . .

NORMAN M. PANITCH, M.D.
San Pedro, CA   United States Public Health Service

10

MODERN MALADIES
Time Deals New Wounds

Medicine doesn't stand a chance of keeping up with contemporary complaints. How can it? Human beings are too inventive, human nature too unpredictable. Germs aren't the only culprit, either. Quite often, twentieth-century lifestyles are to blame. A variety of situations—from watching television soap operas to contending with urban traffic— affect health in painful, silly or surprising ways. Moreover, each season, technological advances designed to make life easier perversely hatch unintended side effects. Modern life breeds modern maladies.

What's required is an antidote for the afflictions of progress. Preventive measures are most efficacious, but there's no vaccination available yet. Therefore, prophylactic treatment prescribes researching the risk/benefit ratio before engaging such modern conveniences as computers, weed eaters, paging beepers, and credit cards. Yes, credit cards. Plastic money may seem benign, indeed a life saver in some situations. But it can be dangerous. People have been known to suffer painful sciatica from sitting on wal-

lets bulging with credit cards. And, a West Coast physician
not only experienced an embarrassing credit-card ailment,
he named it and found a cure.

PLUS ÇA CHANGE, ETC.

To the Editor:

Gould . . . reported three cases of sciatic-nerve irritation
due to carrying a thick wallet in the hip pocket, carrying
several handkerchiefs in the hip pocket, and carrying golf
balls in the hip pocket, a condition that he termed "back-
pocket sciatica." His report seems to represent a general
entity previously described by Battle . . . who reported a
case of sciatica resulting from the carrying of a wallet
stuffed with credit cards in the back pocket. This condition
was termed . . . "credit carditis."

JOHN I. SKOSKEY, M.D., PH.D.

Chicago, IL   University of Chicago

GAUSSIAN CARDITIS

To the Editor:

The cost of serious illness can be astronomical. Such
catastrophic illness can result in financial ruin and subsequent loss of credit. We wish to report another medical
cause of sudden loss of credit: exposure of credit cards to
the magnetic fields in a nuclear resonance scanner.

A patient being scanned . . . began to produce sputum
and had a slight problem in coughing it out of his tracheos-
tomy site. The physician (M.F.R.), who had removed all
metallic objects from his person and had only his credit
cards and wallet in a vest pocket, stuck his head inside the
machine to assist the patient. Four days later the physician

tried to use his card for a 24-hour automatic bank-teller machine, but the card was repeatedly rejected. . . . When he subsequently went to a restaurant, his VISA and American Express cards were both rejected as invalid by the computer-linked credit terminal despite his good credit rating, his previously valid credit, and the usefulness of the cards only one week before.

We wish to call embarrassment due to demagnetization of credit cards "gaussian carditis"* and to warn people who may be involved in the use of nuclear-magnetic-resonance scanners that they should remove not only all metallic objects but all credit cards as well.

MICHAEL F. ROIZEN, M.D.
BARRY ENGELSTAD, M.D.
ROBERT HATTNER, M.D.
University of California at San Francisco
San Francisco, CA   School of Medicine

*NOTE: A gauss is a unit of magnetic flux density.

COMPUTER PROOF OF HUMAN PARTHENOGENESIS

To the Editor:

In the Special Article, "Sexual Behavior in Pregnancy," . . . the authors neglected to amplify the most intriguing bit of data presented. . . . It appears that approximately 1 per cent of 255 pregnant women abstained from coitus before the pregnancy. Although I concede that anecdotal historical precedent exists, I believe that this is the first time that the incidence of immaculate conception has been so scientifically established. However, I caution the medical community that the phenomenon may be confined to Seattle and

further studies are indicated before it can be assumed that
this percentage applies to the United States in general.

ARNOLD ABERMAN, M.D.
Toronto, Canada

*The above letter was referred to the authors of the article
in question, one of whom offers the following reply:*

To the Editor:

Dr. Aberman's letter points out the dangers of transferring interview data to computer cards. The 1 per cent who
abstained from coitus before pregnancy represents one
woman. That woman reported being impregnated by a man
with whom she had no further contact after the conception
of her child. Her partner throughout her pregnancy starting
in the middle of her first trimester was another man. In the
strict sense, she "abstained" from coitus with that partner
before pregnancy. We hope, however, that we have not
diminished Dr. Aberman's faith in the possibility of scientifically documenting immaculate conception in areas other
than Seattle.

NATHANIEL N. WAGNER, PH.D.
Seattle, WA   University of Washington

ABORTION DENIED

To the Editor:

May I cite one example of what the computer may do to
a simple request for payment for medical services? On
three occasions in the past year, the Bradford Group, who
manage the Medicaid program in New York State, have
denied a voucher submitted for a male patient, with the

notation that Medicaid does not pay for abortions.

I have notified them that I do not do abortions, and certainly not in men. Not hearing from Bradford, I wrote a letter to the computer; no answer has appeared.

It is my belief that neither the present nor the future of computerized medical planning should lead physicians and medical educators to the conclusion that it can be as rational or as good as a human brain.

STILES D. EZELL, M.D.
Salem, NY

NO MORE QUESTIONS

To the Editor:

Word processors are remarkable tools, but they may threaten our capacity to question or to register surprise.

Let me tell you how I came into this wisdom. It all began when I turned in the handwritten draft of a paper and asked to have my words processed. In due course the machine excreted a typescript containing the usual quota of errors and two symbols I had not used: "π" had replaced my "?" and "$\pm$" my "!." I had long since submitted to the idea of processed words, but I thought that using standard punctuation marks was still an inviolate right of authorship. That "intimidating machine" (William Safire's phrase) seemed to be challenging what little remained of my free will. Should I tolerate "π" for "?" and "$\pm$" for "!"?

I asked "How come" of the person who had fed my words into the machine. "Oh," came the reply, "I used the 'scientific wheel' for the printout, and that wheel has scientific symbols but no question or exclamation marks." Indeed, that wheel carries the Arabic numerals, the English letters, some mathematical symbols, and a cast of Greek characters. Some computer specialist had, however, liquidated the interrogation point in favor of "π" and the exclamation point in favor of "$\pm$".

Those are dubious trade-offs, since scientists must perforce ask questions. Are the computer people sending scientists a subtle message about future thinkwaysπ. What kind of science or medicine can survive without π. What arrogance exterminated "?" leaving "π" and "$\pm$" to reign. Montaigne was probably wiser than the denizens of Silicon Valley or Route 128, yet his humble motto read, "Que sais-je?" (I presume to use the "?" here.) The scientific enterprise is pointless, except as Mills said in a related context, "To question all things . . ."

I'd sooner a quill pen than surrender punctuation marks to a gadget that acts as if it's smarter than I am. Do you suppose it is π

ELI CHERNIN, Sc.D.
Boston, MA   Harvard School of Public Health

PROBLEMS ON PENNSYLVANIA AVENUE

To the Editor:

We wish to report a side effect of exercise testing with thallium-201, not generally known to physicians, which may result in acute embarrassment for the patient. Over the past few months, in two separate incidents, two of our patients have set off the security alarm system while attempting to enter the White House for the public tour, and each was briefly detained by the Secret Service. Both patients had undergone exercise-treadmill testing with thallium-201 within four days of their White House tours.

Neither patient triggered airport security devices (metal detectors) on their trips from Cincinnati to the District of Columbia. However, both were stopped by the Secret Service when they entered the White House grounds because it was found that they emitted gamma radiation. Each was detained until the cause of the breach of security could be established.

Thallium-201 has a half-life of 72 hours, and a 2.5–mCi dose is used in our laboratory for routine exercise testing. When informing patients of the side-effects of thallium-201 imaging, perhaps a warning against visiting the White House soon after the test should be included.

ROBERT J. TOLTZIS, M.D.
DAVID J. MORTON, M.D.
MYRON C. GERSON, M.D.
Cincinnati, OH   University of Cincinnati Medical Center

LAWN-MOWER ARM

To the Editor:

My case of "lawn-mower arm," which is probably not unique, is yet another of the painful consequences of modern living that have surfaced from time to time in this correspondence column. One of the traps that rotary lawn mowers reserve for the unwary is a sudden catch and arrest of the starter cord, after giving up several inches past the retracted position at which the weekend gardener, having surveyed his unkempt yard, begins a vigorous upward yanking motion, intent on nothing but the nascent chuck-chuck-chuck of this frequently recalcitrant machine. As the full pulling force of the motion is transferred from the starting gizmo to the victim's flexor digitorum superficialis, something inside rips, instantly setting off a burning pain. . . . All flexor movements, especially those of the index and third fingers, become exquisitely painful. Pulling, lifting, and grasping a pen all cause agony, but pushing—even playing the piano—remains virtually painless. The burning pain fades after about three hours, leaving a dull pain and tenderness on pressure, which gradually decrease over the next five days, but finger flexing or scratching motions, particularly with the arm held behind one's back, remain painful longer. Writing is clumsy for about a week. Three to four days after the sprain, a 20-cm yellow patch appears on the volar skin of the forearm. . . . The therapy recommended by this victim is avoidance of medical consultation and continued exercise of the affected limb. In fact, patients unable to tolerate grass taller than 3 inches may exercise the option I chose, i.e., starting the rotary lawn mower with the contralateral hand and mowing while the sunshine lasts.

FRANZ VON LICHTENBERG, M.D.

Boston, MA   Brigham and Women's Hospital

GRASS-TRIMMER'S PURPURA

To the Editor:

I evaluated a 37-year-old white man who had a one-day-old purpuric eruption on the lower part of his legs. The patient had been in good general health and reported only a slight stinging sensation in the purpuric areas. He was taking no medications and had no other symptoms. A physical examination revealed numerous small red and purple macules and papules on the lower anterior portion of the legs between the knees and the dorsa of the feet. . . . The rash was more prominent on the medial aspects of both legs, and it did not blanch when compressed. The eruption stopped abruptly at the ankles and did not involve the feet below the top of the patient's jogging shoes.

My initial clinical impression was that the patient had necrotizing vasculitis, although I could not explain why the rash stopped at the shoe line. After further questions, the patient remembered using a Weed Eater grass trimmer the previous night. He had worn only shorts and jogging shoes while he was working and had ignored the burning sensation caused by the bits of dirt and gravel striking his lower legs. In the light of this information, I ordered no tests. The eruption resolved completely within two weeks. . . .

People who do yardwork do not always wear socks and long pants to protect the lower part of their legs. The distribution of the rash and the patient's history should help in distinguishing necrotizing vasculitis from grass-trimmer's purpura.

WILLIAM M. HENDRICKS, M.D.
Winston-Salem, NC   Bowman Gray School of Medicine

IATROGENIC SOCIOECONOPATHY

To the Editor:

An attractive, bright-eyed young woman of 22 years approached me seeking employment. Her story was interesting in that she was one of the most successful recipients of kidney transplants of a large medical center. She had applied for and was accepted for employment at a local industrial firm. Three days later she was told that they were not able to employ her. When this episode was repeated a short time later, she asked if it was because the firm's medical coverage would be imperilled by her employment, and she was told that it would. She merely wanted me to answer the reasoning behind all the dedicated work of the doctors and nurses and the great expenditure of funds to rescue her from the death pile only to have her relegated to an economic social dump. A case of iatrogenic socioeconopathy?

WILBUR C. THOMAS, M.D.
Meadville, PA

SEASHORE SCIENCE

To the Editor:

During a visit to Florida, I combined business with pleasure by conducting my research on 100 sunbathers. I walked up to them and said I was doing genetic research and wanted to look at their feet. I noted my findings, thanked them, and went on to the next blanket. People repeatedly asked two questions: why I wanted to look at their feet and what it meant, and were they "normal."

An oceanside population offers several advantages to a clinical investigator. In the first place, the people are scantily dressed, and it is not much trouble to examine them (in my case, they did not even have to move). Secondly, they are just lying there, bored, and most are eager to be part of a "medical study." No one refused my request and only one woman asked if I were from Candid Camera. A beach full of people is fairly representative of the general population and is concentrated so that many can be accommodated in a short time. Finally, it combines scientific work with the benefits of salt air and a healthy tan.

An oceanfront population can fit the requirements for various clinical projects—anatomic variations, normal values, public-health and biomedical statistics are a few examples. Even biochemical tests are possible. A sun-bather could be asked to drink a radio-labeled sample and return later to collect a urine sample in the privacy of a tent erected right on the beach.

The people I encountered were willingly examined and interrogated by, and accepted the word of, a barefoot-bathing-suit-clad medico without ever questioning his credentials. I have encountered far more resistance from inhospital patients when attired in my standard white-coat-black-bag-stethoscope regalia. Perhaps a little sunshine in the wards would make them more trusting.

RICHARD E. CYTOWIC
Winston-Salem, NC   Bowman Gray School of Medicine

HAVE A GOOD REST IN THE HOSPITAL

To the Editor:

Recently, one of us (B.A.W.) was hospitalized in our teaching hospital because of a herniated intervetebral cervical disk with radiculopathy. There were no complicating conditions, and the purposes of the hospitalization were the application of cervical traction, the administration of drugs for muscle relaxation and pain relief, . . . diagnostic studies to verify the clinical impression, and . . . physical therapy. The patient kept a diary of interpersonal interactions that occurred during the course of a day. . . . No day started later than 7 A.M. or ended earlier than 10 P.M. Indeed, during the five full and two half days in the hospital, the patient managed only one two-hour nap between 7 A.M. and 10 P.M., and that was on Friday evening.

It is important to note that the patient . . . , except for her cervical disk, is healthy. There were no intravenous fluids to be monitored and no respirators to be tended.

Obviously, these data were collected informally during a

single inhospital experience. We are not aware, however, of systematic studies of this phenomenon and hence feel it appropriate to report these results. . . .

We submit that a hospital, particularly a teaching hospital, is a most unrestful place. The day is long, the harassments are many, though the care is superb. A patient who really needs a rest would do far better to check into a hotel.

A. WILLIAM HOLMES, M.D.
BARBARA A. WINCH
TEXAS TECH UNIVERSITY
Lubbock, TX   Health Sciences Center

TOTAL SATISFACTION WITH SMOKING COUPONS

To the Editor:

. . . All cigarette packages [sh]ould be printed with a detachable coupon. Congress would impose an additional tax that would give the coupon a value of say 10 cents. (Actuarial details can be worked out later.) The coupon would simply state that the holder could turn this in at any hospital in lieu of payment to care for any of the following: carcinoma of the lung, resection or terminal care; most recent myocardial infarction; pulmonary emphysema, chronic bronchitis and respiratory failure; carcinoma of the mouth, tongue, larynx, esophagus or bladder; amputation of either lower extremity; or other ailments as they are identified.

The advantages of adopting such a proposal are many. First of all, it avoids the terror campaign that really confirms the smoker in his practice by letting him openly thwart all those repressive father figures in his psyche (doctors and the Government). And it gives him something for nothing (well, almost nothing), and that is always popular with politicians, even those from tobacco-raising states. Secondly, the Congressmen will think that they've not only acted decisively, but morally. Thirdly, the tobacco industry is nowhere indicted or insulted, and those threats of skull and crossbones have been replaced by an innocuous coupon. Fourthly, the poor epidemiologist trying to compute dose-effect responses can now just count coupons. Fifthly, the socially minded among us will applaud the Government for moving in the direction of great organization for delivery of medical care to all citizens. And lastly, the AMA will be ecstatic because medical care is being provided on a "pay-as-you-go" basis, with the traditional "fee for service."

JOSEPH L. LYON, M.D.
Student
Boston, MA   Harvard School of Public Health

HAZARDS OF A MICROWAVE OVEN

To the Editor:

Medical hazards reported to be associated with microwave ovens include pacemaker dysfunction, burns, cataract formation, and neurologic injury. I describe a case involving another type of injury.

A 51-year-old man with angina pectoris presented with a burn in the area of his Transderm Nitro-10 patch, which had occurred a week previously. He had worn the patches for several months before the burn and has subsequently worn them in other locations without difficulty. On questioning, the patient stated that he was sitting near his mother's microwave oven when she turned it on. He began to experience warmth in the area of the patch, which progressed rapidly, and by the time he was able to pull it off, a burn had occurred. He related that the oven had recently been serviced.

Physical examination revealed a healing second-degree burn on the left side of the chest in the size and configuration of a Transderm Nitro-10 patch.

He was advised to have the oven checked for a microwave leak, and at a return visit, he indicated that one had been found and repaired.

The Transderm Nitro-10 patch is provided with an adhesive strip of aluminized plastic. It is assumed that the metallic element of the patch was heated by microwave radiation, resulting in this patient's injury. Other dermal delivery systems with metallic elements would present a similar hazard.

KENT B. MURRAY, M.D.
University of Kansas
Wichita, KS   School of Medicine

To the Editor:

The advent of the microwave oven has introduced some advantages to the harassed and busy homemaker. I would like to report a serious complication of this technologic advance.

An adolescent patient of mine, ravenously hungry, rushed home from school for his afternoon snack. The first edible item within reach in the freezer was a jelly-filled doughnut, which he promptly placed into the microwave oven for one minute. The outer crust was comfortably warm when he removed the doughnut, which he gulped down in short order. He immediately noticed a searing pain in the region of his upper esophagus. Clearly, the jelly in the center of the doughnut had been heated to a much higher temperature than the covering dough and was hot enough to produce local burns. The symptoms required esophagoscopy. Fortunately, conservative therapy relieved the symptoms during the next week.

ANTHONY PERLMAN, M.B., B.CH.
Baltimore, MD

REFLEX HORN SYNDROME

To the Editor:

I should like to call attention to a medical condition not previously described in the literature, which I have called "reflex horn syndrome," hereafter referred to as RHS. The symptoms consist of automobile drivers, usually the second or third, waiting at a red light who depress their horns for several milliseconds after it turns green. RHS is found predominantly in males, but I do not believe that it is due to a sex-linked inheritance. It occurs almost exclusively in large cities and, in particular, New York. Taxi drivers are particularly prone to RHS.

The importance of RHS is that its cause rests on the . . . stresses and strains that lead to headaches and ulcers. . . . Impatience and frustrations occurring in an urban population that cause the pedestrian to jaywalk, make the driver of a car honk his horn at the first sight of green. Unfortunately, this sets up a vicious circle in that the lead driver becomes angered by the commotion behind him. At the next light, he, in turn, has RHS thereby perpetuating it.

The treatment is a complex one, involving both the individual and the society we reside in. The former has several options open to him, varying from a vacation or three-day weekend to . . . change in residence or livelihood. Treatment of RHS and other manifestations of urban onslaught on a community-wide basis would require that certain amenities be introduced into our way of life. This step would include a cleaner environment, safer streets, improved educational and employment opportunities, housing at a reasonable cost and adequate health care for all our citizens.

SIMEON DAVID, M.B.

New York, NY   Gouverneur Hospital

To the Editor:

It is indeed unfortunate that we inhabitants of Mexico City did not describe the reflex horn syndrome before our colleague Simeon David. . . . As is true of many modern calamities, this syndrome is also seen at this latitude, shamefully at its worst. In the Mexico City area, drivers, men or women but mainly the former (especially taxi, truck and bus drivers) depress their powerful horns (and I mean powerful), several milliseconds before the light turns green; furthermore, they keep doing so until one moves, and many times until one yields the right of way. The reflex horn syndrome in Mexico City may be combined with rudeness of language, gesticulations or flashing of high-beam lights.

I regret that in our city we are beyond any hope of cure or prevention of this rather depressing social disturbance, since the number of such drivers is increasing daily.

GUILLERMO-DE LA VEGA, M.D.

Mexico City, Mexico   Hospital Central Militar

NO SEAT BELT, NO BILLY JOEL

To the Editor:

An estimated 50 percent of motor-vehicle fatalities could be prevented by the use of seat belts. Nonetheless

. . . the majority of people choose not to buckle up. . . . In fact, many go out of their way to disconnect devices that have been installed by automobile manufacturers to promote seat-belt use. Recently, legislation was passed in the state of New York requiring motorists to use restraining devices. We would like to offer a less controversial alternative for improving compliance.

Compared with the general population, drivers between the ages of 16 and 29 years have much higher mortality and morbidity rates due to automobile accidents. Whereas many young adults seem unmotivated to safeguard their health, most seem to have a compulsion to listen to music, which borders on addiction. Our suggestion, then, is remarkably simple. The car radio could be wired in such a way that it could be turned on only by buckling the seat belt. The simplest way to accomplish this would be to remove the on/off switch from the dashboard and place it on the coupling device of the seat belt, with the buckle acting as a circuit breaker. Once the initial reaction had subsided, we believe that young drivers would not think twice about getting into their cars, buckling their seat belts (i.e., turning on their radios), and pulling into traffic. After all, this sequence is already habitual for many motorists, and our modification would be only a minor deviation from the usual pattern of behavior.

. . . Such an approach would be infinitely more palatable than the shrill buzzers, alarms, recorded messages, or legal sanctions currently being used to encourage drivers to buckle up. . . .

JOHN A. CLARK, M.D.
NANCY B. JOHNSON
Salt Lake City, UT   University of Utah Medical School

DON'T OVERLOOK IRON OVERLOAD

To the Editor:

We have recently discovered a potential new, non-invasive screening test for iron-overload conditions.

A 65-year-old white man has been followed in our institution for several years for myelodysplasia with severe erythroid hypoplasia. He requires frequent transfusions of erythrocytes and has received an estimated 300 units over the past four years.

He presented to our hematology clinic in July of this year for a routine visit and incidentally mentioned that he had been unable to pass through an airport metal detector without triggering the alarm. After first triggering the alarm, he was searched, and all metal items were removed from his person. In spite of this, he still couldn't pass through the metal detector without causing the alarm to sound. Airport officials then went over the man with a hand-held metal detector, which reportedly detected metal any time it was in proximity to any part of his body. . . .

Iron overload in this patient is, of course, to be expected. Patients without known iron overload, from whom a similar history is elicited, may deserve investigation.

MICHAEL A. BAUMANN, M.D.
JOSEPH A. LIBNOCH, M.D.
Milwaukee, WI   Medical College of Wisconsin

BAD ADVICE ON DAYTIME TV

To the Editor:

. . . TV's soap-opera character while away hours by wolfing down doughnuts and coffee or swigging alcoholic beverages as they rehash the day's idle chatter or attempt to drown their copious sorrows. The soapland citizens spend a majority of their soap-lives sitting in kitchens, cafeterias, restaurants, and bars, where they appear to indulge ceaselessly in eating, drinking, and gossiping. None ever appears to engage in regular physical activity, except perhaps a few calisthenics at the local health club, while clothed in the latest designer exercise togs and tastefully lacking any sign of post-exercise sweat.

Millions of Americans are as addicted to their favorite soaps as they are to their unhealthy life styles. Sedentary tube viewing coupled with incessant snacking invariably results in "middle-age spread," often before adulthood. . . . Yet, the soap-stars whose lives fans crave to follow appear to be lithe and healthy. Without regard to either diet or exercise, the popular daytime characters are able to look and feel good. Not needing to count up any calories or tie up any jogging shoes. . . . Well-balanced diets and daily exercise programs are generally ignored, and only occasionally will any of the related health conditions—e.g., obesity, high blood pressure, or diabetes—afflict an unfortunate star, usually as a means for character enhancement or as a passing folly forgotten by the next episode.

As a nutrition educator and diet counselor, I object to the misleading implications regarding diet and health imparted to viewers by their favorite television characters. . . .

VIRGINIA ARONSON, R.D., M.S.
Boston, MA   Harvard School of Public Health

FLAT EEG ON TV

To the Editor:

. . . NBC broadcast a program, "The Bold Ones," depicting the miraculous recovery of a young man who supposedly had suffered brain damage in an automobile accident, and who was found to have a "flat EEG" and a "marginal cerebral AV difference." Despite these handicaps he recovered and apparently lived happily ever after, and the hasty young surgeon who wanted the (actor's) kidneys was left a wiser and better man. The clear message to the viewers of this highly dramatic and captivating program is that their relatives with flat EEG's might pull through if they could just stay on the pump a little longer. In their study, "Cerebral Death and the Electroencephalogram" . . . Silverman et al. found from a series of 1600 flat EEG's that such an outcome is tragically unlikely, but there was no hint in this program of the rarity of this phenomenon or its special circumstances (hypothermia or drug narcosis) beyond the fact that it was a "miracle"—the very expression connotes optimism to the faithful. I hope that this program has not spawned an unfortunate epidemic of people who will refuse to believe that their loved ones are really dead, and who will look upon the physician who withdraws mechanical support as a murderer. . . . These programs deal with subjects most precious and important to all . . . and the misconceptions that they implant work to the ultimate detriment of their viewers.

J. H. LOSSING, M.D.

Ann Arbor, MI

ECO-CONSCIOUS DERMATOLOGY

To the Editor:

At this time of heightened environmental awareness I felt quite smug as a private practitioner of dermatology. Surely, my professional impact on the world's ecosystems must be minimal. It was to my horror that I noticed a new antifungal cream containing spermaceti, a whale "by-product." Even more to my horror, I looked closely at the contents of several popular topical steroids . . . to find more spermaceti. There are many excellent topical antifungal agents and steroids not containing any whale by-products, and I should like to urge their use—and to urge a boycott of all companies using products of this vanishing species.

FRED B. BAUSCHARD, M.D.
St. Louis, MO

A GENERIC LETTER

To the Editor:

. . . . We are in an age of depersonalization. . . . We tend not to know our neighbors. . . . We no longer sit on front porches and visit. We no longer walk the sidewalks and talk to each other. We no longer congregate at the neighborhood grocery store or general store. We no longer meet everyone on Saturday in the downtown business district. Many . . . stores, restaurants, and factories are now units of some enormous conglomerate with headquarters in some other, unknown town.

We are also depersonalizing products. We've had impersonal, anonymous, no-name, generic drugs for some time. Now we have generic, no-name beer, as well as generic canned vegetables. . . . The grocery store . . . may have generic meat. This will probably be a compressed roll . . . of turkey, beef, pork, chicken, lamb, or an anonymous combination of all five.

I wonder whether we will soon have generic cars, possibly made in Taiwan. . . . We may have generic baseball teams that will be named just "A" or "B." . . . Movie stars will . . . be replaced by anonymous generic actors. Music will have to be genericized. Songs will be entitled "Oh Beautiful for Generic Skies" or "Under a Generic Moon." Cigarettes will be generic. . . . They will, of course, cause generic cancer.

In Washington we probably will have generic senators and congressmen who will be anonymous and will represent all the people instead of a single state or district. It will be very much harder to catch such generic congressmen at any misdeeds. But the Federal Bureau of Generic Investigation will be on the job, trying to do so. We won't have an army, a navy, marines, or an air force. We will have the United States Generic Military Service. The postal service will have generic stamps with no pictures on them. The tax collectors, called the Internal Generic Revenue Service, will collect generic taxes for generic purposes.

We will go to . . . "The United Generic House of Worship of Whatever." . . . We may have to rewrite the Bible to produce yet another version, which could be called the King Generic Version.

. . . How about calling your magazine "The New England Journal of Generic Medicine"?

PHILIP GENERIC BALL, M.D.
Muncie, IN

SCENTED SOAPS SCOLDED

To the Editor:

I have just finished showering with a "neutral cleansing bar" advertised in professional journals as "superior even to the 'mildest' soaps." . . . Although my skin was not irritated, my nose certainly was; for hours, both bather and bathroom reeked with the scent. . . .

This has caused me to reflect on the daily assaults of our skins, mucosa, and respiratory tracts launched by manufacturers of soaps, cosmetics, tissues, fabric-softener sheets, and disposable diapers. Must everything smell "April fresh," "baby soft," and "close-up fresh," instead of "homey and human"? How many raw baby bottoms, engorged nostrils, and hive-covered faces must we physicians see before we do more than advise patients to avoid these ubiquitous irritants as best they can? . . .

ROSE L. SCHNEIER, M.D.
Philadelphia, PA

CHECK

To the Editor:

An advertisement in the *Journal* depicts two elderly gentlemen playing chess and claims that "Librium rarely affects mental acuity at recommended doses."

It is with regret that I comment that the positions of the black knights and bishop and the fact that the man facing us missed one move in the opening game strongly suggest the opposite.

LESLIE IFFY, M.D.
College of Medicine and Dentistry
Newark, NJ   of New Jersey

"HONEYMOON CYSTITIS"

To the Editor:

. . . Quite independently of the occurrence of urinary-tract infections in women, it is not an uncommon occurrence for a woman with a new sex partner to have a single episode of cystitis after the initiation of a new sexual relation—ergo the name "honeymoon cystitis."

This finding is reproduced over and over again so often that at the Cleveland Free Clinic, where the average patient age is 22 years, when a young woman comes in with symptoms of cystitis, my first question is "Have you recently started a new relationship?" In approximately 80 per cent of the cases, the answer is "Yes." Thus, there is something different about the new relation in terms of producing bacteriuria in females. . . .

MARTIN MACKLIN, M.D., PH.D.
Cleveland, OH   Case Western Reserve University

MALE MEDICAL AUXILIARIES?

To the Editor:

The almost simultaneous arrival in the mail of a letter from my wife's county medical society urging her to make reservations for herself and her wife at the next dinner meeting, and of the ladies program of the spring FACOG meeting in Boston, prompts me to add my own little comedy scene to the ongoing discussion of the subtle problems that confront female physicians and their spouses. The material may not be great, but it has played in cities coast-to-coast over the years.

My wife is a fellow of the American College of Obstetrics and Gynecology. When I accompany her to a national meeting, I go down to the registration desk the first morning, explain how I happen to be at the meeting and ask that, since I am a physician who is not a member of the College, I be given a guest badge. I have invariably been told that guest badges are not available. I then say that in that case, since I am the spouse of a fellow, I want an auxiliary badge, my only purpose being to be able to walk unhindered around the exhibit area. This results in a hurried conference behind the registration desk that ends with my being given the previously unavailable guest badge.

I have never figured out a better way to handle this problem, so I play out the routine each time, having become letter perfect in my part by now.

STEPHEN M. HANSON, M.D.
Wilmington, DE   Veterans Administration Center

11

IT'S THERAPEUTIC
What They Don't Teach in Medical School

Despite spectacular medical advances, home remedies are the comfort of first resort. Miracle drugs are fine in an emergency, but chicken soup is for always. Digital thermometers are state of the art, but Mommy's soothing hand on a child's fevered forehead remains state of the heart. Many old-fashioned treatments are effective and contain a large dose of common sense.

There's a lot to be said in favor of unconventional therapy. In a capsule, it contrasts with patients' pill-popping propensity; it is a salve for the troubled, a tonic for the afflicted. Usually contrived by a lay person or a physician who stumbles upon an original solution to a vexing health-care dilemma, alternative treatments are a tribute to medical ingenuity. Restorative powers of particular procedures— going barefoot to combat forgetfulness, curling the tongue to alleviate a headache—are attested in the Journal's *medical lore. And, if reading about these odd prescriptions elicits a chuckle, that's beneficial, too. According to author and lecturer on medical matters Norman Cousins, laughter is healthful. For, as Dr. Daniel Shindler wrote from Seville, Spain, "The surly bird gets the germ."*

DECREPITUDE PREVENTION

To the Editor:

... Thirty years of experience with hospital, clinic, and nursing-home patients suggests to me that all of us—doctors and nurses included—are haunted by the "specter of decrepitude." Thus, the following information about preventing decrepitude's forgetfulness and incontinence may be of interest.

First of all, forgetfulness often does not appear de novo but is preceded by loss of concentration. Nature, however, appears to have an excellent preventive, that is, by people not wearing shoes. That, of course, seems strange, but consider that barefooted people must continually concentrate on where they put their feet. Observing barefooted children, plus 50 miles of barefooted walking, indicates that if they do not concentrate on where they put their feet, pain from sharp objects immediately signals. Thus, one suspects this primordial biofeedback helps them continually retrain out-of-use neurons to replace dying ones. To the best of our knowledge, populations who go barefooted have little memory loss.

Secondly, loss of bladder and bowel function also often appears slowly. Again, nature seems to have a good preventive, namely by urinary marking of territory. This phenomenon was evident when we confirmed two patients' reports of using their urine to repel cats and dogs. Dogs were invading our garden, urinating and defecating on the plants. The male investigator, therefore, poured urine (sterile) around the garden's edge to see if it would repel the animals. It worked. Then, for scientific completeness, he tried a direct application. One night, clad in sandals and a kilt, he walked the garden's perimeter, urinating a small amount every few steps. Surprisingly, stress on the pubococcygeal muscles was extreme. Therefore, we believe that early people protected their territories using their own urine. Constant use of their pubococcygeal muscles most likely kept their bladders and rectal sphincters strong, thereby preventing incontinence. Similar exercise has been said to ameliorate impotence, hemorrhoids and uterine prolapse.

In conclusion, obeying nature's rules about going barefooted and marking territories with urine may prevent forgetfulness and incontinence, ameliorating decrepitude. However, present customs and laws mitigate against continual barefootedness and publicly protecting territory with urine. One might, nonetheless, advise patients to go barefooted when practical and to do pubococcygeal muscle exercises when urinating. Clearly, nature is an excellent doctor. In fact, it has been said: "Nature can only be commanded by being obeyed."

JOHN M. DOUGLASS, M.D.
SUE DOUGLASS, R.N.
Agoura, CA

FRIGID HEADACHE

To the Editor:

In the light of the recent surge of interest in neurologic esoterica . . . we are compelled to report a therapeutic breakthrough in a heretofore unnamed, poorly understood, yet common neurologic affliction—namely headache, predominantly frontal in distribution, precipitated by excessively rapid ingestion of "slush" or similar products cooled to nearly 0 C.

In a well controlled study of uncontrolled consumption by two senior medical students over a three-month period, the pathophysiology was clarified to our satisfaction. The probable trigger zone of cryogenic cephalgia involves the palatal thermoreceptors, and through vascular response via palatocortical pathways, yields frontal pain. The symptoms were appreciably ameliorated by lingual-recoil therapy, whereby the tip of the tongue is curled back and pressed against the soft palate. The act presumably warms the palate.

R. D. ANDERSEN
A. H. JOHNSON

St. Paul, MN

HOME REMEDIES REVISITED

To the Editor:

A Vermont farmer in his late 50s, an independent and suspicious man, reluctantly presented himself at my office, demanding treatment for upper-gastrointestinal-tract distress. Although his vocabulary seldom extended beyond "Yup" and "Nope," he eventually offered the following story.

He had been evaluated by a cardiologist in distant Burlington some 10 years earlier because of "heart palpitations." He was treated with a drug that "sounded like quinine" (quinidine?) and was relieved of his troubling symptoms. It became clear to him in time that because he no longer had the palpitations, the medication had done its job, and that he no longer needed to take it.

A few months after discontinuing his medication, he awoke one morning feeling weak, tired, and troubled by a persistent sense of palpitations in his chest. To take his mind off his discomfort, he went out to his barn to watch his cattle. As anyone who has ever seen a Vermont farm knows, cattle pens are generally encircled by electrified fencing. When he approached the cattle pen, he stumbled and fell, landing with his chest against the electric fence.

He related that he received an electric shock through his chest, and that his palpitations went away, miraculously.

A few days later, the palpitations recurred, and to be certain that the first episode was not a fluke, he returned to the pen, removed his shoes so that he would be more in contact with the wet grass, and lifted the electrified fence once again to the anterior part of his chest. This time, he related in colorful terms, he had the experience of a syncopal attack. However, when he regained consciousness, his palpitations were once again entirely relieved. He was so thrilled by his discovery that he ran an extension off his electric fence into his basement so that he could relieve his palpitations at will, without having to brave inclement weather.

He refused to accept any advice or treatment for a heart problem that he was convinced was settled. I recommended antacids for his stomach distress, and I never saw the man again.

As remarkable as his story is, what made the greatest impression was that if I hadn't known that an electric shock passed across a chest could effectively resolve cardiac arrhythmias, I most probably would have dismissed his talk as so much colorful folklore. In that context, I have to wonder what other potentially useful therapeutic modalities have been similarly dismissed by me and my learned colleagues.

JERRY H. BERKE, M.D.

Acton, MA

RUMP OVER EARS

To the Editor:

. . . A question of cerebrovascular insufficiency . . . has been teasing me for several years . . . the possibility that the common preference for the upright or recumbent position to a head-down position may be a contributing factor in the very common nerve deafness of old age. I have been toying with the idea for years, ever since I heard a neuropathologist describe the relative inadequacy of the blood supply to the acoustic nerve. Reasoning that our simian ancestors spent minutes if not hours in the head-down position and that various inadequacies in cerebral blood supply might be rectified by imitating them, and in view of the fact that I have occasionally been aware of a blanching of my hearing acuity from time to time, I instituted the simplest of morning exercises, the half-roll out of bed. With head down, count to one hundred. I promptly sense a popping of the ear drums and an inclination to yawn. When I am conscientious about this daily exercise, I am free from any awareness of transient, mild hearing loss. I should add that I am in my middle fifties, and that the curse of my mother's old age was nerve deafness.

Once, describing my morning exercise to a friend, she commented, "So that's why gardeners aren't deaf?" I vacillated. But careful observation reveals that gardeners seldom work with head lower than rump. My mother was a great gardener and she used to mention feeling faint when she stood up from a squatting or kneeling position. Clearly, the brain suffers from inadequate perfusion at such times. I note no similar tendency to feel faint after *my* morning exercise.

PATRICIA WANNING, M.D.
Saugerties, NY

LUNAR CYCLES AND EMERGENCY-ROOM VISITS

To the Editor:

There is a widespread belief among emergency-room personnel that they are busier during the full moon. To determine if there is, indeed, any difference in the number or types of patients seen during the full moon, I analyzed all the patient visits recorded in the emergency-room logbook of the Symmes Hospital in Arlington, Massachusetts, during the 12 lunar months of 1975, recording the total number of patients per day, with separate tallies of patients with traumatic injuries and psychiatric problems, and those who came at night. When these data were arranged in a 29½ day lunar cycle, no pattern was evident.

To analyze these data statistically, I defined the full moon as a four-day period, and compared the average patient census of those four days with the average of the other 25½ days of the lunar month. The observed number of patients in the full-moon period was slightly less than the average for traumatic and psychiatric visits, and slightly more for night-time and total. . . . When I corrected for variation due to days of the week, there was no improvement in statistical significance.

I presented my negative findings to an emergency-room colleague, who retreated to the view that, if patients who come during the full moon are no different in type or number, they are at least "loonier" than usual—and at least etymologically, I cannot disagree.

THOMAS STAIR, M.D.
Washington, DC   Georgetown University Hospital

TREATMENT FOR HICCUPS

To the Editor:

Although seldom more than an annoyance, hiccups can, if it persists, cause great distress. We have observed an exceedingly simple, benign and successful remedy. One teaspoonful of ordinary white granulated sugar, swallowed "dry," resulted in immediate cessation of hiccups in 19 of 20 patients. Twelve of these patients were otherwise in good health, but had suffered from their hiccups for less than six hours and came either to the emergency room or to one of us directly with their complaint.

The remaining eight patients had suffered from persistent hiccups for 24 hours to six weeks; five of them had received other forms of therapy (breathing into a paper bag, phenothiazines) without success. . . . Three suffered recurrence of their hiccups 10 to 24 hours after an initial successful treatment; all responded to repeat treatments (one patient who did not respond did so with a third treatment 24 hours later). Such recurrences are common in the treatment of hiccups and demonstrate the need to seek and eliminate the underlying cause.

A review of the literature of the past 10 years reveals no mention of dry granulated sugar as treatment for hiccups, but we are told that it is known among some lay persons. . . .

EDGAR G. ENGLEMAN, M.D.
University of California
San Francisco, CA　　　　　School of Medicine

JAMES LANKTON, M.D.
BARBARA LANKTON, M.D.
University of Miami
Miami, FL　　　　　School of Medicine

To the Editor:

We read with interest the letter . . . concerning the use of dry granulated sugar in the suppression of singultus. This is in the fine tradition of Mary Poppins, who used a spoonful of sugar in easing peroral pediatric medications. The cessation of hiccups with sugar has been known . . . for at least several generations, and I should like to note that the addition of a few drops of water helps the sugar go down during the administration of this hiccup remedy to younger pediatric patients.

AURELIA D. SCHISEL
ROY H. RHODES, M.S.
University of Southern California
Los Angeles, CA   School of Medicine

To the Editor:

About 20 years ago I learned about granulated sugar for the treatment of hiccups from a Canadian pathologist, of all persons. About two years ago I learned from a lay person what to do when sugar fails. Her remedy is a jigger of vinegar. . . .

GEORGE MARGOLIS, M.D.
Hanover, NH   Dartmouth Medical School

To the Editor:

Hiccups (singultus) have plagued humanity for ages, often at awkward times. Therapy is tedious, with frequent failures. Granulated sugar taken orally has been previously reported as highly effective; it probably activates a local pharyngeal reflex. Hiccups are commonly associated with ethanol ingestion. We wish to report our success with an alternative remedy that is well known to bartenders, but that we cannot find in the medical literature.

All subjects had ethanol-induced hiccups that were unresponsive to traditional treatments. Some subjects were treated more than once, but were hiccup-free for at least one month. Treatment consisted of oral administration of a lemon wedge of the size served in bars; the wedge was saturated with Angostura bitters and rapidly consumed (except for the rind). Small amounts of granulated sugar were occasionally used to enhance palatability, but they did not increase efficacy. Response was defined as at least a two-hour cessation of hiccups with one minute of treatment. The total response rate was 88 per cent (14 of 16 cases), including two cases of initial treatment failure that was overcome after a second treatment within five minutes. These results confirm the anecdotal successes that one of us (D.S.N.) observed while employed as a bartender.

It is unclear from our initial study which ingredient is the active component or whether hiccups not induced by ethanol are affected. . . .

JAY HOWARD HERMAN, M.D.
DAVID S. NOLAN
Baltimore, MD

TREATMENT FOR FLASH BURNS OF THE CONJUNCTIVA

To the Editor:

In addition to being a physician, I consider myself a welder. For many years, I have known firsthand the misery (self-limited though it may be) of occasional flash burns (radiation burns) of the conjunctiva. I have never heard of an effective treatment, though I have tried many. A few years ago I discovered a highly effective treatment that I must share.

The clear gel from freshly broken or cut aloe vera leaf is sterile and soothing; in one or two direct instillations into the affected eye or eyes, it brings rapid total symptomatic relief and seems to speed healing.

DERRY LAWRENCE, M.D.
Corpus Christi, TX

THE THERAPEUTIC VALUE OF SIN...

To the Editor:

One of us (E.P.B.) recently encountered a ... old woman with dementia and chronic obstructive pulmonary disease... recovering from an episode of pulmonary edema. Because of the patient's altered mental status, she was unable to follow verbal commands to cough or to take deep breaths. However, it was noted that the patient could repeat words spoken to her. We took advantage of this fact by singing to the patient, who vociferously sang along with us (the songs included: *Twinkle, Twinkle, Little Star; Hi Ho, Hi Ho, It's Off to Work We Go;* and *You Must Have Been a Beautiful Baby*). While singing, the patient was noted to be taking deep breaths. She also began to cough and expectorate large quantities of sputum. Her clinical status, arterial blood gas levels, and emotional status all improved greatly during this therapy. . . .

EILEEN P. BOLGER, M.S.N.*
New York, NY   The New York Hospital

MARC A. JUDSON, M.D.
New York, NY   New York University Medical Center

OF VEINS, IVS, AND LITTLE RUBBER BALLS

To the Editor:

A 35-year-old woman with chronic relapsing pancreatitis was recently admitted to the hospital. A peripheral intravenous infusion was started, and medication was given for pain. . . .

What made this case remarkable was the ease with which the peripheral intravenous line was started. Just a

...th before, after a number of unsuccessful attempts with the patient's peripheral veins, a subclavian line had been required. The patient had disliked the procedure and—knowing that she would be readmitted sooner or later—had asked if something could be done to avoid this measure in the future.

Upon her discharge she purchased a small rubber ball, which she was instructed to squeeze whenever possible. Within a week she was able to do so 1000 times, although this marathon procedure regularly produced a "burning pain" in her forearm. By the time of her second admission, veins were visibly protruding above the dorsal surface of her hand. She had never noticed these before—nor had I.

Other patients with chronic illnesses and "poor veins" may well profit from such an exercise program.

JAY M. DAVIS, M.D., PH.D.

Arcata, CA

AUTOTHERMAL TREATMENT OF BACKACHE

To the Editor:

The insertion of a heat-reflecting sheet (which can be seen in advertising catalogues) between a sleeper's mattress and his bedsheet will demonstrate the large amount of heat produced by the back of his body. I found that such a sheet provided a nightlong heat pack that was reasonably efficient. Perhaps I am displaying my ignorance, but I have never seen this simple treatment for backache mentioned.

IRVINE H. PAGE, M.D.

Hyannisport, MA

Plantain Leaf for Poison Ivy

To the Editor:

The itching associated with poison-ivy dermatitis can be mitigated or stopped when the crushed leaves of the common plantain, or plant herb (*Plantago lanceolata*, narrow leaf; *Plantago major*, broad leaf), are rubbed on the affected areas of the skin. We used narrow-leaf plantain. Plantain can grow profusely on any lawn in the United States. This treatment, part of the Maryland Eastern Shore folk-medicine tradition, was suggested to me by a Georgetown, Maryland, resident, Mr. Peter Monk, because I had suffered acutely and repeatedly from poison-ivy dermatitis.

A group of 10 people—family and friends, all sensitive to poison ivy—were treated with plantain. . . . The treatment was repeated up to four times in some cases, but the itching stopped in all cases, and the dermatitis did not spread to other areas of the body. This treatment is a blessing for those who must have a constant supply of calamine lotion or cortisone during the warm months. There was little scientific objectivity in this clinical experiment and there were no controls; the patients were told of the past therapeutic successes of plantain.

. . . The therapeutic effects of plantain have been known at least since the 16th century. The following conversation is from Shakespeare's *Romeo and Juliet* (I.ii.52–3):

ROMEO: Your plantain leaf is excellent for that.
BENVOLIO: For what, I pray thee?
ROMEO: For your broken shin.

SERGE DUCKETT, M.D., PH.D.
Philadelphia, PA   Jefferson Medical College

SIMPLE CURE FOR NOCTURNAL LEG CRAMPS

To the Editor:

Most of us have been inconvenienced by at least one nocturnal calf cramp. Many of us will at some time experience this symptom frequently enough, without apparent underlying illness, to be placed among the mass of victims of recurrent, idiopathic nocturnal calf cramps and to share their scramble from bed and efforts to find relief by means of stretching, massage or hot soaks. Episodes result in loss of sleep, sore muscles aɪ̩d an occasional broken leg. Many technics have been recommended for cramp prevention, . . . some of which, including the use of magnets under one's mattress, seem bizarre. None of these approaches have had their effectiveness established. . . .

We have recently treated 44 adults with frequent recurrent cramps (eight of them reported at least two cramps every night for the preceding three months) by means of a simple stretching exercise. Patients were instructed to stand with their shoes off, face a wall two or three feet away and then lean forward, using the hands and arms to regulate their forward tilt and keeping the heels in contact with the floor until a moderately intense, but not painful "pulling sensation" developed in their calf muscles. The stretching position was held for 10 seconds, then repeated after a five-second period of relaxation. This sequence was repeated three times daily until all leg cramps were gone, then used with whatever frequency was necessary to maintain a cramp-free state.

Twenty-one of the 44 patients reported disappearance of their symptoms within 24 to 72 hours. All reported cure within a week, and all have remained nearly cramp-free for follow-up periods of as long as one year, without preventive therapy. Some continue to stretch daily, but many stretch infrequently and only in anticipation of a cramp—

for example, after strenuous exercise. Many have taught the technic to friends with similar symptoms, who have apparently found it successful. . . .

                                HARRY W. DANIELL, M.D., F.A.C.P.
Redding, CA

WIG FOR SEIZURES

To the Editor:

I should like to offer a tip how patients with seizure disorders can be helped. I find that female patients with seizure disorders may be protected from head injuries by having them wear the thick wigs so popular these days. A wig padded with foam rubber works even better.

                                MICHAEL J. FAELLA, M.D.
Warwick, RI

UNICYCLE SEAT TO SPARE PROSTATE

To the Editor:

My cardiologist has advised me to commute on a bicycle, but my urologist has forbidden the practice. Here is a practical problem that might face any man in his forties. For the sake of his coronary vessels, he should ride a bicycle; for the sake of his prostate gland, he should not. In my case, the dilemma was confounded by strong feelings about the automobile and its effect on the environment: noise, traffic, air pollution, proliferating highways and the oil lobby.

The solution to my immediate problem became obvious one day when I was visiting a bicycle shop. I happened to notice a unicycle seat, and it occurred to me that this concave, dumb-bell-shaped object could be mounted transversely in the place of an ordinary bicycle seat. Set at the proper angle and suitably padded, it would support the torso on the ischial tuberosities without putting any force on the perineum.

I purchased the unicycle seat for $5, and . . . the device is a complete success. With a minimum of technical skill and ingenuity, any cyclist can replace the unhygienic saddle with a comfortable seat that spares the perineum. . . .

RONALD W. ANGEL, M.D.
Stanford, CA   Stanford University School of Medicine

KING TUT'S REVENGE

To the Editor:

The Gorback editorial properly cites the symptomatic relief that Pepto-Bismol can provide for travelers' diarrhea. It also notes the inconvenience of carrying several bottles of this product in luggage. Perhaps it isn't widely known that Pepto-Bismol is available in the form of chewable tablets. . . . On a recent trip to Egypt I was hit by King Tut's Revenge and secured immediate relief from the tablets, which I carried in my camera case. I chewed one every half hour, while awake, during the first day of symptoms and one every hour for the next few days. Movements were promptly reduced to one or two per day for the balance of our stay. . . .

RICHARD K. BERNSTEIN, M.D.
Valhalla, NY   Westchester County Medical Center

SUPPRESSION OF SALIVATION IN WIND-INSTRUMENT PLAYERS

To the Editor:

A vexing problem for recorder players is the accumulation of moisture in the recorder's windway. This occurs particularly in better instruments copied from original prototypes, which had narrow, tapering windways. Even a small droplet will cause burbling, loss of volume, and notes that will not speak.

Since most of the moisture is saliva, a pharmacologic agent that suppresses salivation should be helpful. I have tried and had excellent results with the recently available transdermal preparation of scopolamine (Transderm-Scop). . . . I have found a marked diminution of salivation within 15 minutes of application, which persists as long as the patch is worn and for about half an hour after its removal; I had no other side effects. The patch can be reused, since it is too expensive for a single use and is designed for three days of motion-sickness control. . . .

CARL E. DETTMAN, M.D.
Waban, MA

PSEUDO-ENURESIS RECUMBENS

To the Editor:

. . . A 53-year-old man noted three separate episodes of enuresis over a four-day period. He had awakened with wet pajamas and bed-clothes but no other indications. His pajamas were wet only over his buttocks and groin, and his wife, who slept in the same bed, was not wet. He denied having dysuria, urgent or frequent urination, fecal incontinence, or back pain. The results of a complete physical examination were normal.

He was referred to a urologist. However, before his appointment he noted a small leak in the filler port of his mattress; the leak occurred only when he applied pressure to the mattress. Since the patient was heavier than his wife, the water trickled to his side of the bed only, and since his buttocks were the lowest part of his body—at least in bed—it trickled to them.

The patient repaired the leak and the enigmatic enuresis ended.

GARY REGALBUTO, M.D.
PAUL HAMADA, M.D.
Hood River, OR

IF YOU SNIP, DON'T ZIP!

To the Editor:

We are a manufacturer of zippers. It has recently come to our attention that at least one physician is using our zippers to close surgical incisions.

Our products are not designed or manufactured for medical purposes and were never intended for such use. In addition, our product is not sterile or packaged or manufactured in a medically sterile environment. During the manufacturing process our zippers are in contact with or made with oils, lubricants, detergents, dyestuff, and other common chemicals. The finished product is not hazardous if used as it is intended to be used. Therefore, illness or injury may result if this product is used for surgical purposes.

We urge *Journal* readers not to use zippers for medical purposes. We cannot be responsible for any injury caused by such use, and we disclaim any warranty, expressed or implied, in connection with medical use of our products.

BERNARD J. RUBIN
Macon, GA YKK (U.S.A.)

The above letter was referred to Dr. Harlan Stone, who offers the following reply:

To the Editor:

The use of the zipper has greatly facilitated reexploration of the abdomen when it is required on an almost daily basis. We have tried many different zippers over the past few years. Our initial studies used the YKK, but at present we prefer the Talon, since it is less likely to disengage spontaneously and lead to evisceration.

H. HARLAN STONE, M.D.
Baltimore, MD University of Maryland

THE NEED FOR SUBSPECIALISTS (AUTOMOTIVE DIVISION)

To the Editor:

My wife's car, now in its middle age, recently acquired an anginal syndrome characterized by insufficiency of gas flow in exertion (e.g. acceleration) relieved by rest (idling fine in neutral). The symptoms were complicated by trepopnea (worse on left turn) and generalized sluggishness. The primary-care practitioner at the local service station couldn't put his finger on the problem right away, so he recommended a "tune-up" (or as he called it, a "complete"). However, the infusion of $80 provided only temporary relief of the symptoms, and within a few weeks, there was a complete relapse. Despite several more office visits to the generalist for minor refinements of therapy, and several home remedies (pouring a can of this or that into an appropriate orifice), the symptoms continued unchanged.

Our local paper runs an automotive advice column in which it printed a letter describing a case similar to my own. The auto doctor made a suggested diagnosis of "carburetor trouble." Taking out the yellow pages, I readily located an appropriate practitioner (specialty, engines; subspecialty, carburetors), who took a detailed history and then attached the leads of an impressive electronic machine to various spots on the engine and performed an electrocabogram (ECG). The trouble was soon detected, minor surgery was performed, and the patient was dramatically improved at a cost less than half that incurred at the generalist.

I've had similar experiences with transmissions and squeaky noises from the front end, as we all have. Subspecialists have always seemed to handle these problems more efficiently and more economically than generalists. They ask the right questions, they have the right tools at hand, and they inspire greater confidence in consumers of medical care. Training programs for practitioners of automobile repair would seemingly do well to encourage the production of more specialists, while continuing to train generalists as well. The problem is to identify and implement routes of referral that will lead the patient who needs a subspecialist directly to a practitioner appropriate for the ailment.

ROBERT A. GREENWALK, M.D.
Long Island Jewish–
Hillside Medical Center

New Hyde Park, NY

12

POSTMORTEMS
In Story and History

*Seeking a second medical opinion and peer review take on
new meaning in the pages of the* Journal, *where physicians
render fresh diagnoses on case histories from biblical
times and exhume many a* corpus delicti *that never had a
real body in life. Hindsight, particularly if there's evidence
of foul-play, often leads medical sleuths on a merry chase
through literature and myth for the solution to a mystery.*

*Take the case of poor Arthur Dimmesdale, dead these
many years, yet unable to rest in peace. Literary critics
generally have attributed the demise of the errant reverend
in Nathaniel Hawthorne's* The Scarlet Letter *to powerful
guilt neurosis. Yet no medical file is ever truly closed; on
rereading the classic, Dr. Jemshed A. Khan at the University of Missouri–Columbia volunteered a new diagnosis.
He charged, "The poisoning of a major character in a
widely read novel, written by a celebrated author, has
escaped forensic detection for more than a century. This
should be of interest to the medical community, because the
poisoning was accomplished through the agency of a phy-*

213

sician." Newspapers pounced on the story with zeal, as if it were the latest testimony in a lurid criminal trial.

Dr. Kahn agreed with literary critics that the nineteenth-century murderer was Dr. Roger Chillingworth, Dimmesdale's physician. Citing passages from the novel, Khan presented evidence that Hester Prynne, the adultress, also suspected her estranged husband. Certainly Chillingworth had a motive, revenge. Dimmesdale had cuckolded him. In addition, Dr. Khan pointed out, the physician, a "practiced alchemist," had the means as well as the opportunity. From a locally grown plant, Dr. Chillingworth could have concocted the poison, atropine, whose symptoms Hawthorne details in the novel.

Several second opinions were offered in response to the new diagnosis. Some colleagues complained that turning Hawthorne's classic into a mystery story trivialized the book. But Dr. Khan countered, "Everybody knows whodunit; the question is 'howhedunit.'"

Atropine Poisoning in Hawthorne's *The Scarlett Letter*

To the Editor:

The article by Khan entitled "Atropine Poisoning in Hawthorne's *The Scarlet Letter*" . . . makes some ingenious, hard-earned points in arguing that because the Reverend Dimmesdale fathered a child of Hester Prynne, her husband, the physician Chillingworth, administered atropine poison to Dimmesdale, his patient—which "accounts for . . . the ultimate demise" of the clergyman. . . .

Hawthorne . . . upset Dr. Khan's thesis. When Dimmesdale is dying at the end, old Chillingworth cries, "Thou hast escaped me!" Is it necessary to point out that no mur-

derer could put such a complaint to his victim? Chillingworth did not want Dimmesdale dead and very soon
"shrivelled away" himself. Hawthorne does say that there
were those who thought that an *A* that appeared on the
minister's breast in the end had been effected by the physician's "poisonous drugs." But he adds that those best able
to understand Dimmesdale did not think so; "the tooth of
remorse" had caused it.

PHILIP YOUNG
University Park, PA   Pennsylvania State University

To the Editor:
    . . . The theme of the physician as poisoner is prominent
in a earlier Hawthorne work as well. In 1844, six years
before the publication of *The Scarlet Letter*, Hawthorne
published "Rappaccini's Daughter," a short story about a
Paduan physician who keeps his daughter, Beatrice, isolated in a private garden of poisonous plants. As an experiment, Rappaccini gradually poisons her so that she
acquires a physical dependence on the poison yet maintains
her health. The plot develops as Giovanni, a medical student, tries to court Beatrice and gradually realizes that her
breath and touch are deadly. His loved one's embrace
would mean certain death. . . .
    Ultimately, Giovanni gives Beatrice an antidote in an
attempt to liberate her. . . . However, because of her physical dependence, Beatrice dies poisoned by the drug that
should have cured her: atropine, the antidote for aconitum.

KARL D. KIEBURTZ
University of Rochester
Rochester, NY   School of Medicine and Dentistry

To the Editor:

. . . For those who argue that Dr. Khan's assertions are faulty, let me suggest that Hawthorne was aware of the herbs and poisonous plants of his day. . . . In his book *Hawthorne's Mad Scientists*, Stoehr contends that Hawthorne was aware of the homeopathic theory advanced by Hahnemann in 1790, which "was largely devoted to the description of drugs and to the rationale for their selection and administration." . . . *The Scarlett Letter* abounds with references to deadly nightshade (atropine), as well as henbane, wormwood, dogwood, apple-of-Peru, and the like, all of which are highly toxic.

VIRGINIA MCCORMICK
Allentown, PA   Allen High School

To the Editor:

. . . Many of the symptoms Khan submits as proof of atropine poisoning began before Dimmesdale met Chillingworth. . . . Although Chillingworth was a vengeful physician well versed in plant lore, he did not want to kill Dimmesdale but to torment him. What has long interested members of the medical community is Chillingworth's perverse application of a psychoanalytic method: aware that bodily disease can result from "some ailment in the spiritual part," he exacerbates the minister's guilt by urging confession. . . .

RITA K. GOLLIN
State University of New York,
Geneseo, NY   College at Geneseo

To the Editor:

The message of Hawthorne's *The Scarlet Letter* does not have to do with poisoning but with the effect of the emotion of guilt on the physical well-being of the patient. Several statements by Hawthorne make this point repeatedly. One . . . "Whenever there is a heart and an intellect, the diseases of the physical frame are tinged with the peculiarities of these."

The physician's role was to torture the emotions of the guilty minister, not to poison him. . . .

. . . And finally, how could a man whose mind was disturbed by poison and whose speech was impaired by atropine preach an acclaimed . . . sermon minutes before his self-willed death?

ANDREW KERR, JR., M.D.
Hudson, OH

To the Editor:
As a nonphysician reader of the *Journal*, I frequently find myself relying on medical friends for a more precise understanding of the material discussed in each issue. Not so with Dr. Khan's article. I am a student of literature and count *The Scarlet Letter* among the works I have researched and written about myself. Dr. Khan provided a refreshing twist to Hawthorne's work. Gone is the heavy symbolic or allegorical structure put forward so often by literary scholars. The reader is left with the kernel of a possible truth rather than the chaff of rhetoric that only leads to more questions. . . .

I would have been completely convinced if the article had not come to its "rash conclusion." Though Hawthorne may have known, through his extensive reading about atropine, that a "rash may appear, especially over the face, neck, and upper part of the trunk," he took a real symptom and masked it in symbolic interpretation. For among the crowd who witnessed the Reverend Dimmesdale's demise (or said they witnessed it), there were those who saw something (an *A*) and there were those who saw nothing. So the learned doctor or the literary scholar is left with the red rash of atropine or the red badge of Dimmesdale's inner agony or nothing at all. The ultimate interpretation is the reader's own.

BARBARA STORMS
Chicago, IL   University of Chicago

HAWTHORNE AND PERICARDIAL CALCINOSIS

To the Editor:

Hawthorne surely must have been medically sophisticated. The fate of Ethan Brand's remains, for example, may equally be taken for illness or allegory:

> Within the ribs—strange to say—was the shape of a human heart. "Was the fellow's heart made of marble?" cried Bartram, in some perplexity at the phenomenon. "At any rate, it is burnt into what looks like special good lime, and, taking all the bones together, my kiln is half a bushel the richer for him."
> So saying, the rude lime-burner lifted his pole, and letting it fall upon the skeleton, the relics of Ethan Brand were crumbled into fragments.

This was written less than 100 years after Morgagni's first medical report of pericardial calcification. Subsequently, pericardial calcinosis was named *Panzerherz* by the Germans, and this description would fit what they have called "*ausgesprochene Kalkpanzer.*"

DAVID H. SPODICK, M.D., D. SC.
University of Massachusetts
Worcester, MA   Medical School

To the Editor:

. . . What critics have known for centuries is that attention must be fixed on the symbolic meaning of any poison that has been aligned by Hawthorne with the darker side of nature, alchemy, and medieval science.

Hawthorne was a writer of romance, as the original subtitle of *The Scarlett Letter* makes clear. He could have specified the kind of poison as Flaubert did in *Madame Bovary*, in which the heroine dies of strychnine.* . . .

MARCIA ZORN
The University of Dayton

Dayton, OH

*NOTE: Professeur Guy Vourc'h, Institut d'Anesthésiologie, Paris, offered a second opinion. "Madame Bovary, in Flaubert's famous novel, committed suicide by using . . . arsenic, and Flaubert provides quite a good description of the symptoms. . . ."

SUSPICIOUS CIRCUMSTANCES IN SALEM

To the Editor:

In the editorial by Donaldson . . . the challenge of hereditary angioedema is discussed, and our awareness of this disease is traced back to the family of Pyncheon, who resided for many generations in the House of the Seven Gables. This surprising literary interpretation stimulated my own return to Nathaniel Hawthorne's book, in which Colonel Pyncheon is cursed by Matthew Maule as follows: "God will give him blood to drink." As I remembered, the victims of sudden death in this family were all found frozen in the position of their last activity on earth, with blood on their ruffs, shirt bosoms, and hoary beards.

The evidence of hemoptysis or hematomosis is certainly most unusual and unexpected in hereditary angioedema. I appreciated the opportunity to reread Hawthorne, but I disagree with the posthumous diagnosis of their sudden deaths.

SONIA STUPNIKER, M.D.

Philadelphia, PA

David, Goliath and Smiley's People

To the Editor:

For some time we have puzzled and anguished about one aspect of a particular story in the Scriptures: How did David slay Goliath? The story is, of course, familiar to everybody, but certain new "facts" have come to light. The armies of the Philistines and the Israelites were gathered in the vale of Elah. The Philistines had challenged the Israelites to let the war be decided by the outcome of a contest between two warriors, one from each side. The champion of the Philistines, Goliath, appeared. His height was 6 cubits and a span. He had a helmet of brass and was clad in a coat of mail. He was armed with javelin and spear. King Saul was distraught because his policy of deterrence was in shreds. He called in his chief of staff, his national security advisor, and other experts. The consensus was gloomy: the Israelites' chances were zero! In despair, someone suggested calling in George Smiley from Intelligence. Smiley studied Goliath's profile carefully. Something jogged his memory.

"I will need some time," he said softly.

He left and went to find Connie, the human computer, armed with her favorite bottle.

"Connie, what do we have on giants in Canaan?"

"Well," she said, "there was the story that Joshua brought back about families of giants."

"What happened to them?"

"They all became ill. Some went blind, others bled or slipped into coma, and they all developed soft bones —soft as butter, Georgie!"

Smiley hurried back to Elah and was immediately given an audience with Saul.

"We have only one opportunity," he declared. "Choose a youth swift and skilled with a sling!"

The choice was obvious, as Michelangelo's statue will attest: David, son of Jesse.

"Use no armor," said Smiley, "but come in from the side so he won't see you, and hit him in the forehead."

And David took a stone, slung it, and smote the Philistine. The stone sank into his forehead, and he fell to the earth. David went on to become a great king of Israel, owing in large part to Smiley's insight into what lay behind Goliath's armor—a classic example of multiple endocrine neoplasia Type 1. Smiley's people had put it together this way: Goliath had acromegaly, and the pituitary tumor was probably so large that it produced homonymous hemianopia (eyewitnesses said Goliath had to look about to find David). He also had a pancreatic tumor, but it was uncertain whether it secreted gastrin or insulin. He may have been hypoglycemic on the morning of the contest, but it was hyperparathyroidism that killed him. He had extensive osteitis fibrosa with a brown tumor on his forehead, through which the stone pierced his brain.

DAVID RABIN, M.D.
PAULINE L. RABIN, M.D.
(with apologies to John le Carré)
Vanderbilt University
School of Medicine

Nashville, TN

To the Editor:

John le Carré might have detected an inaccuracy in the confrontation of David and Goliath as depicted by Rabin and Rabin. . . . The large pituitary tumor probably produced a bitemporal visual-field defect, not a homonymous hemianopia; and if there was papillomacular-bundle involvement, Goliath may have been hampered by central scotomata as well.

Perhaps the dust of the battlefield also obscured the view, since another description credits Elhanan with the slaying of Goliath.

L. L. COVELL, M.D.

Wakefield, MA

L. M. COVELL, M.D.

Brookline, MA

To the Editor:

To reassure Covell and Covell . . . and in defense of King David: The dust of the battle probably only confused the copyists. Some Hebrew manuscripts and the Septuagint include the words "Lahmi the brother of" between "Elhanan slew" and "Goliath."

T. J. HAMBLIN
Bournemouth, England   Royal Victoria Hospital

To the Editor:

Even before Smiley's people diagnosed the case of Goliath, a similar diagnosis had been made by Dr. Robert B. Greenblatt. [*Search the Scriptures: Modern Medicine and Biblical Personages*, 3rd ed. Philadelphia: J. B. Lippincott, 1977.]

The only major difference is that Greenblatt suggests that "as Goliath hesitated, clumsily turning his head to bring back the youth within his limited field of vision, David . . . took deadly aim with the slingshot and struck the lone spot unprotected by heavy armor."

NAOMI E. TORREZ, M.L.S.
Vallejo, CA   Kaiser Foundation Hospital

The above letters were referred to the authors of the original letter, who offered the following reply:

To the Editor:

Covell and Covell's point is well taken. We checked with our "sources" at Smiley's Circus, who stated that their information was that Goliath's optic chiasm was pre-fixed. The tumor thus compressed one of the optic tracts, which accounted for the field defect. Strictly off the record, they incline to the view that human error was involved and that "homonymous" was inserted instead of "bitemporal."

Ms. Torrez correctly reminds us that many people had previously deduced that Goliath had acromegaly. We would like to acknowledge the work of Jackson [Jackson, C. E., Talbert, P. C., Caylor, H. D., "Hereditary hyperparathyroidism," *J. Indiana State Med. Assoc.* 1960:1313–6], which we learned about only recently. He figured it all out without the aid of John le Carré!

DAVID AND PAULINE RABIN
Vanderbilt University
Nashville, TN   School of Medicine

ELISHA'S BEDSIDE MANNER

To the Editor:

I found the analysis by Dr. Gordis of physician-patient interaction in the Elisha-Naaman story both delightful and thought provoking. . . .

May I suggest that the physician's (Elisha's) avoidance of direct contact with the patient (Naaman) was both purposeful and necessary to attain the entire therapeutic goal? The goal included not only the cure of the physical disease of leprosy but also spiritual healing as evidenced by that astounding monotheistic confession from a Syrian polytheist: "Behold now, I know that there is no God in all the earth, but in Israel."

Elisha seems to have taken preventive measures to keep his patient from becoming dependent on him, the intermediary, rather than upon the One Who alone wholly heals. At the same time, he demonstrated that one receives the benefaction of God without regard to status or position, but contingent on precise adherence to the Divine prescription.

Such principles are worthy of consideration by us as physicians who subscribe to the concept of treating the whole patient.

JOHN D. VAN DER DECKER, M.D.

Norfolk, VA

To the Editor:

I thoroughly enjoyed the comments by Dr. Gordis interpreting the Old Testament treatment in modern terms. I would argue with the validity of his concluding two sentences. Nowhere in the story is a warm bedside manner demonstrated, nor is it used as a substitute for cure. Physicians with the competence of Elisha may use cure of disease and relief of symptoms in lieu of a warm bedside manner, but the rest of us should try to develop competence in all three endeavors to maximize patient satisfaction.

TERRY F. DYNES, M.D.

Docorah, IA

HOW ABRAHAM LINCOLN DEALT WITH A MALPRACTICE SUIT

To the Editor:

The following article, published in the Bloomington *Daily Pantograph*, Bloomington, Illinois, on July 5, 1931, describes a malpractice suit against doctors who were defended by Abraham Lincoln in 1856. It was two years before the Lincoln-Douglas debates and four years before Lincoln's election to the presidency. . . .

The first suit for malpractice that was filed in the McLean Country Circuit Court had as defendants Drs. Crothers and Rodgers. The plaintiff was Samuel Fleming. The most interesting feature of the action was the presence of ABRAHAM LINCOLN as attorney for the defendants. . . . The physicians knew Lincoln well. The nurse who had taken care of Lincoln's children had also served the children of Dr. Crothers and there were other bonds of friendship.

As the records show, Mr. Fleming fractured a leg and engaged the two defendants to set the bone. The break was a bad one, and the knitting process slow and when completed it developed, as is said to be the case with elderly patients, that the limb was a trifle shorter than it was before. Holding that the two surgeons had not given the fracture proper attention, Fleming sued them for malpractice. Lincoln was sent for and agreed to take the case. He was then living in Springfield and came up to Bloomington on several occasions to be coached upon the subject of broken bones. The two surgeons, both distinguished in their profession, used a chicken bone to explain the different conditions in bones of young people and those of advanced age. In the former case the bone has a springy, wiry condition less apt to break and a tendency to knit quickly. In the case of old people the bone is more brittle while the lime and other qualities impair the knitting qualities. The physical characteristics of bones were explained to Lincoln in minute detail and when the coaching was completed he knew about as much on the subject as the physicians themselves.

When the suit finally came to trial, Lincoln argued the case using the chicken bone and other illustrations. He concluded a brilliant argument by saying: "Mr. Fleming, instead of bringing suit against these surgeons for not giving your bone proper attention, you should go on your knees and thank God and them that you have your leg. Most other practitioners with such a break would have insisted upon amputation. In your case, they exercized their skill and ability to preserve it and did so. The slight defect that finally resulted, through Nature's methods of aiding the work of the surgeons, is nothing compared to the loss of the limb altogether."

The President-to-be threw his whole soul into the defense, and the jury promptly brought in a verdict for the defendants, and threw the costs, reaching a large figure, on the plaintiff.

CLARK HEATH, M.D.

Rockport, MA

B. FRANKLIN VS. OLD WIVES ON COLDS

To the Editor:

Evidently, the "commonly held belief that exposure to cold influences or causes common colds"... has been viewed skeptically by learned men for hundreds of years. No less a person than Benjamin Franklin was interested in this question. In a letter from the year 1773 he notes... "colds are totally independent of wet and even cold."

With the literature of the day seeming to support his opinion, he did "propose writing a short paper on this subject...." However, he must have been rather careful for he further states that his opinion about exposure and colds was a "Hersey [heresy] here, and ... I only whisper it...." So acute were his powers of observation that he further wrote on the topic that "people often catch colds from one another ... and when sitting near and conversing so as to breath in each others' transpiration." Unfortunately, the proposed paper ("Prepatory Notes and Hints for Writing a Paper concerning What is Called Catching Cold") was never written but, as noted by William Pepper, was "the nearest approach to a real medical article among Franklin's writings."

Although it is comforting to have Franklin's convictions confirmed by modern science, it is also comforting to realize that with keen powers of observation one may arrive at similarly held beliefs.

EDWARD WM. GERNER, M.D.
Neurology Resident
Hospital of the University
Philadelphia, PA   of Pennsylvania

EDITORIAL COMMENT: The Journal *acknowledges that priority belongs to Benjamin Franklin—by some two hundred years! Further excerpts from William Pepper's book have just been published in* Medical Affairs *of the University of Pennsylvania, issue of October, 1968, and these establish Franklin's precedence without question.*

At Brunswick, but one bed could be procured for Dr. Franklin and me, in a chamber little larger than the bed, without a chimney and with only one small window. The window was open, and I who was then invalid and afraid of the air of the night, shut it close. "Oh," says Franklin, "don't shut the window, we shall be suffocated." I answered I was afraid of the evening air. Dr. Franklin replied, "The air within this chamber will soon be, and indeed is now, worse than that without doors. Come open the window and come to bed and I will convince you. I believe you are not acquainted with my theory of colds?"

Opening the window, and leaping into bed, I said I had read his letters to Dr. Cooper, in which he had advanced that nobody ever got cold by going into a cold church or any other cold air, but the theory was so little consistent with experience that I thought it a paradox. The Doctor then began a harangue upon air and cold, and respiration and perspiration, with which I was so much amused that I soon fell asleep and left him and his philosophy together, but I believe they were equally sound and insensible within a few minutes after me, for the last words I heard were pronounced as if he was more than half asleep.

I remember little of the lecture, except that the human body, by respiration and perspiration, destroys a gallon of air in a minute; that two such persons as we were now in that chamber could consume all the air in it in an hour or two; that by breathing over again the matter thrown off by the lungs and the skin, we should imbibe the real cause of the colds, not from abroad, but from within.

"NATURE AND NURTURE" IN SHAKESPEARE

To the Editor:

The excellent editorial, "Nature and Nurture," by Harris . . . and the equally stimulating article by Blass and Gibson on an inborn enzyme abnormality leading to susceptibility to the Wernicke-Korsakoff syndrome caused me to search my memory for what may be the original expression, "Nature-Nurture." It is from Shakespeare's *The Tempest*, Act IV.

Prospero, the deposed Duke of Milan, has spent many years on an island. He has raised and tried to teach the servant Caliban from a child born of:

> The foul witch Sycorax, who with age and envy,
> Was grown into a hoop.

Prospero was unsuccessful in teaching Caliban, whom he calls a "beast," "a freckled whelp hag-born" and "this mis-shapen knave." Caliban plots against his master and Prospero meditates:

A devil, a born devil, on whose nature
Nurture can never stick; on whom my pains,
Humanely taken, all are lost, quite lost;
And as with age his body uglier grows,
So his mind cankers.

We have gained in our understanding and care of our "exceptional" children and our Calibans. It is of interest, however, that it was a poet many years ago who expressed insight into what is of great concern today.

CLARK W. HEATH, M.D.
Rockport, MA

EERIE MURDER IN SHAKESPEARE'S *Hamlet*

To the Editor:

The article by Drs. Eden and Opland . . . proposes that the murder of Hamlet's father by the pouring of "hebenon" in his ear was suggested to Shakespeare by the rediscovery of the eustachian tube in 1564. Although this may be correct, the concept of medicinal drugs and poisons entering the body by way of the ears was widely held in England by the time *Hamlet* was written (1601). Several of the widely distributed herbals of the 16th century, which were compendia of the therapeutic as well as the botanical knowledge of the era, described this. As early as 1525, the herbalist Banckes mentioned two drugs that could be used to treat disorders of the brain and stomach when they were administered as a "juice dropped in the ears."

The "cursed hebenon" of Shakespeare's *Hamlet* was probably not a fictional drug. The poison henbane, obtained from plants of the hyoscyamus species and also recorded in the 16th-century herbals as "Hannebane," was probably the substance referred to by Shakespeare. The descriptions of symptoms of henbane poisoning in these herbals are similar, although not identical, to those described by the ghost of Hamlet's father, and they indicate a belief that henbane was a very penetrating drug. The herbalist Langham said that to "wash the . . . eares" with henbane seethed in wine will induce sleep.

EDWARD TABOR, M.D.
Bethesda, MD

To the Editor:

R. R. Simpson, in his authoritative book *Shakespeare and Medicine*, points out that poison instilled into the ear was not new: "Ambroise Paré was wrongfully accused of murdering Francis II of France by blowing a poisonous powder into his ear." Francis died in 1560. Christopher Marlowe, Shakespeare's eminent predecessor, in his *Edward the Second* (produced in 1590) has Lightborn tell how murder can be accomplished: "Or whilst one is asleep, to take a quill,/ And blow a little powder in his ears" (5.4.34–5). The play *Hamlet* was entered in the Stationer's Register in July 1602.

Simpson goes on to quote from several articles written by David I. Macht, once professor of pharmacology at John Hopkins. Macht, an active Shakespeare buff, experimented with various alkaloids, instilling them into the external ears of animals. He demonstrated that a number of poisons—aconitin, nicotine, belladonna, hyoscyamus, and conium—could be absorbed through the intact eardrum.

Macht found that hyoscyamus, belladonna, conium, and aconitin all produced marked shortening of the coagulation time of the blood, which may explain the report of Hamlet's father's ghost (1.5.68–70):

> And with a sudden vigour it doth posset
> And curd, like eager droppings into milk,
> The thin and wholesome blood; so did it mine.

It seems likely that Eustachio's discovery may not have been the only source of Shakespeare's presentation of poisoning through the external ear.

EDWARD SHAPIRO, M. D.
Los Angeles, CA

DID FALSTAFF HAVE THE SLEEP-APNEA SYNDROME?

To the Editor:

Recently, while listening to a reading of *Henry IV*, First Part, I was particularly intrigued by a brief section in Act II, Scene IV. After concealing Falstaff's presence from the sheriff, Prince Hal calls for Falstaff. The lines are as follows:

> PRINCE: This oily rascal is known as well as Paul's. Go, call him forth.
> PETO: Falstaff! Fast asleep behind the arras, and snorting like a horse.
> PRINCE: Hark, how hard he fetches breath. Search his pockets.

In recent years we have documented in profuse detail the abnormal breathing pattern of obese patients whose upper airway is obstructed during sleep. I think Shakespeare sums it up quite neatly in his lines "snorting like a horse" and "Hark, how hard he fetches breath."

Chest physicians and physiologists have shown their literary bent by coining the term "Pickwickian." May we now label the problem of heavy breathing among an increasing number of obese people the "Falstaff snore" or the "Falstaff syndrome"?

JACK J. ADLER, M.D.
Brooklyn, NY   Brookdale Hospital Medical Center

FALSTAFF WAS DRUNKER THAN HE WAS FAT

To the Editor:

I write to rescue Shakespeare's Sir John Falstaff from the ignominy of unwanted eponymy. . . . Dr. Adler attributes Sir Jack's snoring and hard fetching of breath while sleeping to obesity. Not so! This rendering is deficient in failing to record Falstaff's most notable personal characteristic and the single most pertinent aspect of his "history": Falstaff was a chronic drunk. The scene in question . . . at the Boar's Head Tavern finds Sir Jack thoroughly "potted," as was his wont, from near continuous imbibing of cups of "sack" (sherry). He passed out in an adjacent quarter, where he was found by the Prince and Peto, snoring mightily. I have it on some authority that even a skinny man, when sufficiently perfused with spirits, will so snort in his stuporous repose as to disturb another's slumber. Cure is effected by an intervening day of sobriety. Sir John, to the discerning reader, was not nearly so fat as he was drunk. "Falstaff syndrome," indeed. Fie!

R. P. JUNGHAM
Miami, FL   University of Miami School of Medicine

WHAT THREE THINGS DOES DRINK PROVOKE?

To the Editor:

The findings presented by Gordon et al. . . . on the effect of ethanol on testosterone metabolism were anticipated by an early worker, William Shakespeare, in 1606:

MACDUFF: What three things does drink especially provoke?
PORTER: Marry, sir, nose-painting, sleep and urine. Lechery, sir, it provokes and unprovokes. It provokes the desire, but it takes away the performance: therefore, much drink may be said to be an equivocator with lechery: it makes him and it mars him; it sets him on, and it takes him off; it persuades him, and disheartens him; makes him stand to and not stand to; in conclusion, equivocates him in a sleep, and giving him the lie, leaves him [Macbeth, Act 2, Sc. 3.]

ALEXANDER HANNENBERG
Boston, MA   Tufts University School of Medicine

ADOLF HITLER: HIS DIARIES AND PARKINSON'S DISEASE

To the Editor:

It is known that Adolf Hitler had Parkinson's disease. This has been noted by Hitler's own physician, Dr. Theodore Morrell. The evidence is best illustrated by the description in Stolk's "Adolf Hitler: His Life and His Illness" [Stolk, P. J. "Adolf Hitler: His Life and His Illness," *Psychiatr. Neurol. Neurochir.* 1968; 71:381–98]:

. . . he developed a tremor, which probably affected only the left side. It was first noticed in his left arm (autumn of 1942) and subsequently also in the left leg. . . . It is of course possible that this tremor had developed much earlier but had . . . escaped notice. His left arm was kept hanging down trembling heavily, or was pressed against his body and he dragged his left leg; the upper part of his body tended to incline forward, and finally he was unable to walk without supporting himself. . . . In fact it was for this very purpose that he had benches spaced along the walls of the great bunker which was his final retreat. Standing up, he was forced to grab hold of his partner in conversation for support. His speech was low-pitched and hardly intelligible. His facial expression became rigid and mask-like, and saliva occasionally escaped from the corners of his mouth. In his final years, Hitler was quite evidently suffering from parkinsonism.

There has been much interest recently in the discovery of several handwritten volumes that were purported to be Hitler's diaries. These diaries have been shown to be forgeries on the basis of a detailed chemical analysis of their paper, ink, and binding. If the diaries had been written by Hitler, then the later ones would probably exhibit micrographia. Hitler's micrographia may be evidenced by the change in his signatures between 1932 and 1944, as shown.

Hitler's Signatures in 1932 and 1944
(Courtesy, *Newsweek*)

Along with several of my colleagues at the New York University Medical Center, I had the opportunity to examine the first (1932) and the last (1945) of the diaries before the forgery was exposed. Although there is a change . . . the handwriting does not exhibit micrographia. Nonetheless, its absence was, to us, evidence against the diaries' authenticity.

ALFRED N. LIEBERMAN, M.D.
New York, NY

"TIN DRUM SYNDROME"

To the Editor:

The articles concerning emotional deprivation and growth retardation . . . fascinated me, particularly because of the analogy one can draw between the children in the study and the "hero" of *The Tin Drum* by Günter Grass. In this excellent satire the protagonist, Oskar, stops growing at the age of three in response to the attitudes of the adult world about him. Like the children in the study, Oskar engages in much antisocial behavior—from the continual pounding of his tin drum to breaking plate-glass windows with his voice. Günter Grass's emotionally provoked dwarf became so by force of will—even to the point of providing the adult world with a medical excuse for his shortness by deliberately falling down stairs. Oskar's reasoning is contained in the following passage:

> I remained the precocious three year old, towered over by grownups but superior to all grownups, who refused to measure his shadow with theirs, who was complete both inside and out, while they to the very brink of the grave were condemned to worry their heads about "de-

velopment," who had only to confirm what they were compelled to gain by hard and often painful experience, and who had no need to change his shoes and trouser size year after year just to prove that something is growing.

One would need to be at least half facetious to suggest that the children in Powell's study are willfully short, and yet the analogy, although possibly not perfect, suggests that the naming of this process is the "Tin Drum Syndrome."

MICHAEL E. BLAW, M.D.
Associate Professor of Pediatrics and Neurology
University of Minnesota
Minneapolis, MN   Medical School

SUPERFECUNDATION AND SUPERFETATION

To the Editor:

In the second-century Talmud (Tractates Yebamot and Niddah) we find discussed the possibility that one woman can be pregnant at one time from two men—i.e., superfecundation. Since conception occurs within three days of cohabitation, states the Talmud, if the woman copulates with another man during this period, mixing of the sperm may occur, and the child may, in fact, have two fathers.

Also discussed in the Talmud is the possibility that a pregnant woman will become pregnant again from a later cohabitation—i.e., superfetation. Even earlier than the Talmud, Aristotle (*De Generatione* 4:87) and Hippocrates assumed that a human uterus has two horns; one horn was thought to become pregnant first, and then the other horn at a later date. In his classic book on Biblical and Talmudic medicine [Julius Preuss, *Biblical and Talmudic Medicine*, edited by F. Rosner. New York, Hebrew Publishing, 1978, pp. 386ff, 417ff], Preuss points out that superfetation is possible in the very rare case of a complete duplication of the female genital tract. In the normal uterus, however, stuperfetation might occur during the first month or two of pregnancy but not later. Such an opinion is already expressed in the Talmud. For a more detailed presentation of this subject and for precise bibliographic citations, the interested reader is referred to Preuss' book.

FRED ROSNER, M.D.
Queens Hospital Center Affiliation
of the Long Island Jewish–
Jamaica, NY   Hillside Medical Center

MARLEY'S HEAVY CHAINS

To the Editor:

"Heavy-Chain Disease" . . . was reported in 1843 by Dickens in "A Christmas Carol." If not the first report, this was perhaps the best-known early account of persons afflicted with heavy chains. Marley dragged a heavy chain composed of "cashboxes, keys, padlocks, ledgers, deeds, and heavy purses wrought in steel." A second characteristic, Jacob Marley's transparent body, allowed the observer to verify that this phantom had no bowels, as it had often been said during the shade's lifetime. As sleepy fat boy Joe is linked to the Pickwickian syndrome, may Jacob Marley become the best-known and earliest documented case of heavy-chain disease!

JOHN B. DE HOFF, M.D.
Baltimore, MD

To the Editor:

The letter from Dr. De Hoff . . . calling attention to the picture of Marley's disemboweled ghost in Dickens' "A Christmas Carol" (1843) serves also to note that the artist, John Leech, had been a medical student and an apprentice to a pair of London practitioners before taking up his career as an illustrator. Ten years previously he had trained at St. Bartholomew's Hospital under Edward Stanley, who was both a surgeon and an anatomist. It was Stanley who noted Leech's skill in drawing during his anatomy lessons, and who probably suggested a career as an artist rather than that of a surgeon. Leech, therefore, knew his anatomy inside out and may have even seen, without recognizing the syndrome, examples of "heavy-chain disease," while walking the wards of Bart's with Mr. Stanley!

HENRY R. VIETS, M.D.
Boston, MA

To the Editor:

With reference to Dr. De Hoff's claim . . . for Jacob Marley as "the best-known and earliest documented case of heavy-chain disease," I doubt if it was well advised to have started a journey down this road. I am afraid you will be flooded with claims of priority and interest. Perhaps not antedating Jacob Marley but possibly even better known was the contemporary case of Dumas's Edmond Dantes, the Count of Monte Cristo, who not only suffered from an episode of heavy-chain disease but also effected his own recovery and permanent cure.

Certainly, regarding both priority and interest, and far antedating both Marley and Monte Cristo, as well as Franklin's reported patients, a good case can be made out for Prometheus, whose heavy-chain disease was complicated by repeated severe hepatic trauma. Of especial interest is that his is undoubtedly also the first description on record of partial hepactectomy and ensuing hepatic regeneration.

ARTHUR M. GINZLER, M.D.
Pathologist
Warren, OH   St. Joseph Riverside Hospital

THE TIGHT-GIRDLE SYNDROME

To the Editor:

During the last year or two I have become acquainted with the tight-girdle syndrome, which has fascinated me. It arises from the attempts of a rather stout woman to contain herself within some bounds of shapeliness. It has three aspects that have brought it to my attention. First of all, on a number of occasions I have been puzzled by finding a vigorous carotid pulse accompanied by a jugular pulse visible just about the edge of the right clavicle. The rest of the examination of the patient has shown no physical abnormality of the heart or blood vessels to explain this unusual pulsation in the neck. But when on occasion I have asked the patient to loosen the girdle, this pulsation has disappeared, much to my satisfaction and relief and to that of the patient, too, who now breathes more easily and feels less choked up.

The second aspect of the syndrome is gastrointestinal, with a displacement upward of diaphragm, stomach and esophagus, causing symptoms that are often attributed to a hiatus or diaphragmatic hernia with or without heartburn and gaseous eructation and commonly called cardiospasm. Again, loosening of the girdle relieves some of the symptomatology.

And, thirdly, it is quite obvious on fluoroscopy to see that the diaphragm is pushed up, and the heart displaced upward to assume a horizontal position with a decrease in the thoracic space for the function of the lungs and of the heart. Dyspnea can result, relieved again by loosening of the girdle.

The tight-girdle syndrome is doubtless a residual of the popularity for the wasp waist that was in style a couple of generations ago, featured in many of the fashion magazines of the epoque. Perhaps now that women have been liberated they may also be free of the feeling that they need tight girdles.

PAUL DUDLEY WHITE, M.D.

Boston, MA

To the Editor:

... Samuel Thomas von Sömmerring (1775–1830), the great Prussian anatomist, described this syndrome in a monograph published in 1788.

Morton's annotated bibliography of the history of medicine states: "Sömmerring enumerated the bad effects of tight corsets on the internal organs of women. His paper created much interest and resulted in a great decline in the fad of tight lacing and hoop skirts." ... Therefore, we believe the "tight-girdle syndrome" should be called "Sömmerring's syndrome."

JOY ANN BELL, M.D.
GEORGE CARTER BELL, M.D.
University of Texas
Health Science Center

San Antonio, TX

SÖMMERRING'S SYNDROME? NO! NEVER!

To the Editor:

. . . Sömmerring's treatise on the dire dangers of the corset, brought about by a lessening of the practice of tight lacing, is factually wrong. On the contrary, the practice of tight lacing, which had almost disappeared under the influence of the French Revolution, revived and began to gather steam just after the appearance of the second edition of Sömmerring's notorious work in 1802. This fashion continued to intensify in Europe and the United States until it reached its peak shortly before the turn of the century. All in all, it lasted more than a hundred years longer than implied in Morton's bibliography.

The public burning of the corset by German students at the Wartburg Celebration did indeed take place in 1817, but, alas, it was a man's corset that was committed to the flames. . . . The students and an assorted bevy of older German nationalists chanted the following verse in unison on that occasion.

> A corset girds with great élan
> The waist of every proud Uhlan.
> So that when he in battle stands
> His heart won't fall into his pants.

One reason why Sömmerring does not deserve the honor of having a syndrome named after him is that he attributed cancer, tuberculosis and scoliosis to the wearing of corsets by women. . . .

GERHART S. SCHWARZ, M.D.

New York Eye and Ear Infirmary

New York, NY

ABOUT THE EDITOR

SHIRLEY BLOTNICK MOSKOW, a graduate of Boston University College of Public Communications, is a free-lance writer with a special interest in medicine. A former newspaper reporter and editor, in 1983 she was the first woman elected president of The New England Chapter, Society of Professional Journalists. In addition to medical publications, her articles have appeared in national magazines and major metropolitan newspapers from coast to coast. She also teaches writing workshops at Middlesex Community College in Bedford, Massachusetts. She lives in Lexington, Massachusetts, with her husband, Richard. They have two sons.

HERE'S TO YOUR HEALTH!

A compendium of useful titles from Fawcett Books.

TAF-54